Healing
In His
Wings

Gregory R Reid

ACKNOWLEDGEMENTS

Cover Photo by Anthony Francois Photography
http://www.photosbyafb.com/

Many thanks to Anthony and Margaret Barrerras for their great work on the cover.
God bless you in all you do!

CONTENTS

Gregory R Reid

FOREWORD

In 1983, I began a 15 part series called "Healing in His Wings." For many years, I saw less and less of books and articles that really addressed the needs of the heart for believers. We were becoming more knowledgeable, but I wasn't sure we were getting healed of our wounds, nor getting a greater glimpse of who God wanted us to be. I wrote the series to address these needs. In the years since I wrote that series and sent it out to the small and important group of friends and supporters that have kept me afloat all these years, I have also, from time to time, written other things from the heart - and sometimes of a prophetic nature, and made them available as well.

One of my favorite verses – and the reason for the title of this book – comes from Malachi 4:2a: "But unto you who fear my name shall the sun of righteousness arise with healing in his wings…" As most believers, I took the analogy to be about God through Jesus being like a big feathered wing taking us under and heal us. And, maybe that's it. But I heard someone familiar with Hebrew and Jewish customs that suggested that the wings are actually referring to "edges" – the edges of the Jewish Tallit or prayer cloth that every Jewish believer wore – including Jesus – and that the "wings" were the fringes of it. Then I remembered the woman who was so ill she literally was crawling and who said, "If I can only touch the hem of His garment I will be healed." A more accurate read would be, "If I can only touch the edge (fringes or tzitzi) of His Tallit (prayer cloth) I will be healed."

Suddenly I found myself touched to the heart with the reality that just to touch the very end of His prayer cloth was enough to heal the humble heart. Thus the cover.

I offer these to you for the first time in complete form. I pray that they will bring you into a deeper walk with God, a greater sense of your purpose, and a sweeter sense of His nearness and love.

Gregory R Reid
Winter, 2013

1 WHERE ARE THE DAVIDS OF GOD?

They are among us in multitudes, in our midst and outside our walls. They are silent victims, social lepers, the object of painful jokes and an embarrassment to the socially proper. They are afraid to reach out and too hurt to risk another rejection. They are a part of us. They are a reflection of us.

Once, I taught a Bible study on unconditional love. How I loved to preach it! Nobility is so much easier talked than walked. Accept the outcast! Love the unlovely! The first person to approach me after the study was an unkempt, mentally challenged man who said, "Will you have coffee with me?" It was like God saying, "O.K. Greg, you preached it, now will you do it?" I didn't want to. I was scared. My reluctance surfaced so much selfishness, so many questions and fears. I did go with him, in a group of others, but I really failed the test and have failed it since. Unconditional love: So easy to preach. So painful to learn.

She came into the coffee house we were working out of in the Tenderloin of San Francisco. She smelled so bad it was difficult to get within five feet of her. One brave girl sat her down, gave her a sandwich and shared Jesus with her. The lady was overwhelmed by the love of God, for she knew the pitiful condition she was in. She accepted Jesus, and died days later in a hospital, her body eaten away by a disease. Could I have reached out to her? I wonder to this day.

They are always there after I preach a service. They wait on the back rows while those who least need to talk reach the front first. A sad face, a lonely man, lingering for a while, afraid to come forward, desperate for help, afraid of rejection, or worse - being ignored. They were there before I came to speak and will be there after - for weeks, months or years, or until they are snatched away by Satan, or just drop out of sight, unnoticed, unloved.

Let's face it - we tend to cater to the lovely and those easy to minister to. "Problem people" are easy to ignore, and too often when they fall away, we pass it off with a smug, "They must not have been right with God." But I'm beginning to believe that if Dietrich Bonhoeffer's words are true, that "We must learn to regard people less in the light of what they do or omit to do, and more in the light of what they suffer," then we should fear to judge those who fall away because we failed to love them.

Forgive me if I appear oversensitive to such people, for I was one. I made it to 15 by sheer miracle because the deck was stacked against me. Beaten down, depressed, a scarred face, I had faced many battles and lost them all. I accepted Christ - my life changed - but I failed to find the loving Christian I needed so much. I was ignored, hurt and even kicked out of one church. I was ready to give up. I was bitter, frightened and alone. God's promises meant nothing. They were for others, not for me. Then a little white-haired Baptist lady came into my life. She didn't care what I looked like. She didn't care what sins I'd committed or what horrible things I'd done.. She looked beyond the exterior defenses and self-projected ugliness and saw my desire to serve Jesus despite my wounds and sins. When I saw a frog, she saw a prince in me. She was committed to me becoming that prince enough to patiently endure stumblings, hurt and failure. SHE NEVER GAVE UP! As I sang at her funeral in 1977, I thought, "I'm here because you cared. You endured. You showed Jesus to me when I could not see His face."

You see, we live in a time of unprecedented emotional wounding. There are those who have been abused by their father who consider seeing God as Father frightening and impossible. Our counseling to such is often cold and terse: "Do this. Read this verse. If you don't, don't come back." We don't realize some people are dead inside and CANNOT do it without the breath of God being breathed into them by a caring believer. We get frustrated with problem people and say, "Grow up!", not realizing they can't grow up without a miracle of healing from God.

Consider with me for a moment the kind of people God calls worthwhile. Jacob was a deceiver. "Righteous Lot" was guilty of incest. Jeremiah was full of self-pity. David was a murderer and adulterer. Jesus rejected those too self-full to see their need, and chose a prostitute, a tax-gatherer, a ruthless con artist (Zaccheus) a betrayer (Peter) and a host of other sordid characters. Why? Because He knew, before THEY knew, that they of all people needed Him most.

Our age differs only in prevailing need. In Jesus' time, doctors were scarce and sickness rampant. Now we have doctors and medicine, but few for the diseases we face: Loneliness, fear, occultism, family trauma, fragmented hearts. We have yet to see the healing power of Jesus in these areas as we shall.

But, back to the title: Where are the Davids of God? The Elijahs have preached judgment, and we have no doubt needed it. But to some, it brought fear and wounding, for they were already afraid of God. They can't receive grace because they hide their sins in fear of more rejection.

There is a very small story in the life of David that has gripped me to my very soul. You'd miss it if you weren't looking for it. David, mighty king, full of wealth, all his enemies subdued under him. Lover of women, anointed of God, respected by multitudes: What else could he ask for? I can see him on his mighty throne, wistfully thinking of his beloved Jonathan slain in battle. Jonathan: his covenant brother whom David had loved more than his own life. He calls in his counselor: "Is there anyone left of Jonathan's family I can show kindness to?" There was, and he was hiding. He had good reason to, as his father and grandfather and family were all dead. When he was just a baby, his house was under siege, and his nurse picked him up, and in fleeing, dropped him, leaving him crippled for life. He was bitter and afraid. "Son of a king, hah! David, the great king, took my place! I should have been king!" His name was Mephibosheth.

David sent for him, and Mephibosheth was no doubt confused and terrified. Life had already dealt him the cruelest of blows. Was this the final cruelty, death at the hand of a usurper-king? But the unexpected awaited him: A weeping king, overwhelmed at the sight of the son of his beloved Jonathan. Not judgment, but arms of love and kindness; not death, but grace. David pulled out the stops. Mephibosheth was to be as David's own son, eating at his table, blessed with all provision, cared for, the rest of his life.

WHAT A REVELATION! Beloved, there are thousands of Mephibosheths among us. They are crippled, afraid and alone. They see the privileged and blessed as usurper-kings and they are bitter. We preach the blessings of God to them, but they only say, "It's for you, maybe, not for me." We tell them what to do, but fail to walk through the Dark Valley WITH them!

I recently spoke with a friend whose life had dealt him more cruel blows than most people dream of in their worst nightmares. He struggled, failed, almost gave up. He was filling out a test, and one question was, "Give one word your best friend would use to describe you." He said, "That's easy. You're the friend; the word is prince." When I hung up the phone, the tears fell. O God, one word of all my words brought hope! Prince! Faith that failure was not final and the end result was royalty!

David had a covenant with Jonathan: "All I have is yours." We have that covenant with Jesus. David longed to extend that covenant of blessing to Jonathan's son. Because of our covenant with Jesus, our heart should cry to reach out to the crippled Mephibosheths in our midst to extend that covenant to them, saying, "All I have is yours!" Yes, they are crippled, bitter and unlovely. But we have a covenant we must fulfill, remembering we were once ugly ourselves. There are paupers without hope who believe the best life offers is temporary relief from excruciating pain. But they are princes in the heart who just don't know it yet, and God awaits our next move.

The Spirit of Elijah, partially fulfilled in John Baptist, would "Level the high places and exalt the valleys to make straight the way of the Lord." I appreciate the mountain-leveling, it has been necessary to humble the proud and destroy the spiritual loftiness in our midst. But we also need to raise up those in the valley of despair. Paul understood this: "Who is weak, and I am not weak? Who is offended and I do not burn with anger?" (2 Cor. 11:29) When is the last time YOU went to bat for a weak believer who had been wounded by a proud or insensitive believer? Paul also made it clear that the unlovely members deserve the MORE abundant honor! Are we seeking to fulfill that command? Where are the Davids of God? The Mephibosheths I know in multitudes, and I am only one seeking to extend the inheritance.

But where are the Davids of God? Yes, it is costly, time-consuming, patience-trying. But to repeat a word a friend once shared, "The church is useless unless it is ready to get coffee spilled on its rug." There are prostitutes waiting to become princesses. There are the crippled who can become long-distance champion runners. There are outward failures who have the potential to become mighty men of valor. But they await the extending of God's covenant through us.

15 years ago I gave my life fully to Jesus at a house meeting. I struggled and failed. But I kept trying, while I watched scores of my Christian friends fell away. After leaving Bible school I attended a coming home party for the man who directed the house meeting I was saved in. He said, "Some who started so strong are not even with the Lord. But look at Greg; he was such a mess. I wouldn't have given you a plug nickel he'd still be with the Lord." But I was, because ONE PERSON extended God's inheritance to me, and would not let me be anything less than the prince I was born-again to be.

There are those of you that think you can never be anything but a failure. Your Christian walk has been one big mess, one failure after another. Let me share a word a pastor-friend of mine gave that changed my life: "You can be a great fourth-quarter Christian. It doesn't matter how you start the game: IT'S HOW YOU FINISH." God has called you to be sons and daughters of the King of Kings. God doesn't see your crippling or failures: He sees your heart. You are loved beyond your wildest dreams. God made you so you would inherit the stars. Put away all your self-loathing and bitterness. His best promises are for you. YOU! Dare to believe in your spiritual adoption birthright and put on your royal robes. Let the lowly be exalted. Let the weak say, 'I am strong!' You were born again to be princes and princesses in your Father's house!

The Spirit of the Lord searches the church. "Who will go for us?" WHERE ARE THE DAVIDS OF GOD?

Gregory R Reid

2 NOTHING IS TOO GOOD TO BE

"Why do dreams have to die?" Have you ever asked yourself that question? But dreams don't have to die - not if they are God-given dreams. Much has been taught on the "death of a vision." And in one sense, dreams DO have to die, but we too often stop short of seeing the full glory of God's purposes.

We all have dreams and desires. We want to be someone. We want to be emotionally whole. We want to do a great work for God! We want friends. Sometimes God Himself gives the dream or vision. So it was with Joseph. When he was a boy, he dreamed all his family came to him as their leader. For an insecure headstrong boy, that was heady stuff! And where did it lead? To betrayal, a dungeon and despair. Have you been there?

Most of us would have become bitter. "God, you lied! You promised, and you let me down!" But Joseph stayed faithful and looked to God. In a time of confusion and turmoil, he did what the scriptures wisely tell us: "Trust in the Lord with all your heart, and lean not on your own understanding; in all your ways acknowledge Him, and He will direct your paths." (Pr. 3:5,6) If he had leaned on his own understanding, he would have concluded God a liar. If he had leaned on the arm of his flesh, he might have said, "If I were God, I'd get me out of here NOW!" And if he had gotten out when he in his own wisdom thought he should, he would have ended up a forgotten man on the streets of Egypt. But because he trusted God rather than his own understanding, the death of his dream was not the end! In one day, he was set free and became the second most powerful man in all of Egypt. God fulfilled his dream!

DEATH IS NEVER FINAL

There are important lessons to learn here. First, death is never the final note for the believer. Christians fear death because they can't understand it. For us, death is not the end, but the door to more life! Death has no power over us, for once we are alive in Him, death is only a step to everlasting life. In our daily life, when we are faced with "death" to some thing or some one, some dream or desire, it's too easy to stop there. "Suffering is all there is. All life is death." As dangerous as it is to deny suffering as a real and valuable part of our walk, it is equally destructive to deny joy and fulfillment and life! God is not a dream crusher. He's a dream fulfiller! But we must remember - God is a dream sanctifier, and that is where the death comes in.

15

A father may intend to give his son all he has, in time - but he would be insane to give his five year old the keys to the family car. He's not mature enough to drive yet. God says, "You are My heir" and we want to jump behind the wheel! God stops us and we cry, "But You said! You promised!" God isn't crushing the dream, He is developing it, and you. He's protecting your inheritance by delay, and we won't see the fulfillment until we trust His wisdom and timing completely, and above our own.

"Death" to a dream is merely its sanctfication. We don't live in death. There is power in the cross, but do not forget the empty tomb! Too many see God as a taker, insensitive to our pain. How wrong we are! He is a giver, and when He DOES take, it is only so He may give us more, to give us eternal things! Paul said, "I die daily" but he didn't live in or dwell on the death. He just let go of the temporal and lesser to receive the eternal and greater! Joseph merely experienced death to his immature, selfish view of the dream God gave him so he could receive the greater fulfillment of his dream.

SECOND BEST

If Joseph would have trusted his own understanding, he would have been robbed. Many of us, trusting our own understanding, do the same. There is much truth to the saying, "God gives the best to those who leave the choice to Him." But HE must choose. "He shall choose our inheritance for us." (Ps. 47:4) Some live in destruction because they have no sense of worth and would turn down a blessing even if God gave it. Others grossly overestimate themselves ("I deserve the best!") and trade eternal riches for things that perish. We do either of these because of a lack of trust in our loving Father. Those who demand prosperity and those who settle for false martyrdom are both separated from trust. We must put our love and attention on Him, knowing that He will never do us wrong.

We also settle for second best regarding holiness and wholeness. We want an easy out. It's easier to pray, "God change that person" or "change my situation" than "change me." God did not take away Joseph's situation until it had worked a glorious work in him for the eternal best! If I demanded, I think God might change my friends, environment and position. But I might remain the same selfish, short-sighted person. But if I change and become a whole person, it won't matter to me if things change, and things will change because I'm not drawing destructive things to myself anymore. God's best doesn't mean easiest, but it does mean concrete and eternal. The other is just a Band-Aid. Paul said, "God has given us richly all things to enjoy." He didn't say, "God has given us ALL THINGS richly to enjoy." It isn't abundance that matters, but attitude. Before, I was unhappy because I wanted more recognition, admiration and material things. But the more I had, the more miserable I was! But as wholeness has come, suddenly every little thing I have is a treasure, one friend a wealth. A sunset was a cinema event, and a kind word was a gold nugget. God wanted to fill and heal me, but I had to trust HIS ways over my own.

DESIRES OF OUR HEART

"But God said He'd give me the desires of my heart," you cry. Consider two things here. First, He does give us the desires of our heart - He literally gives us the things HE desires for us! God doesn't give us what we childishly want, but He literally gives us the desire that will be HIS desire, if we let Him!

The second matter involves letting Him change our desires. Some time ago I was looking for a place to house my ministry. I wanted a mobile home, because it seemed ideal to me. But after a week of looking, an opportunity to purchase a house came up. Suddenly the mobile home seemed impractical and undesirable. While I bid on the house, I decided a house purchase was impractical and a financial burden I didn't need. I decided to rent. That is something I wouldn't have considered at first. The place I found was practical, affordable, and a wise investment - everything I needed. Because I prayed and put my heart's desire in God's hand, He matured me in the process so that my desire matched His wise best. What I thought I wanted and needed was not God's best at all! God changed my desire to fit the long-term best.

Joseph may have felt his dream should have been fulfilled right away. He wanted recognition, love and respect. But in the prison, he was matured and inwardly strengthened, and he was ultimately fulfilled. His childish, selfish interpretation of God's dream became, in the crucible, the salvation of all of Egypt and the restoration of his own family. When a child says, "I want to be a doctor," he has no idea what it will take - schooling, disciplining, waiting. When God gives us a dream, He knows we cannot comprehend the end goal. That is why the PROCESS is so critical to God. He is more concerned with the process than the goal, because it is the person's maturity that judges how he will fare, not the profession he is to take. And only selfish parents are bent on the child's profession being what pleases the parent above and over the child's growth and fulfillment. God is more concerned with our relationship with Him, our growth and maturity than in what we can do for Him. When your dream meets with God in the crucible of change and maturity, you will become all He wants you to be, and more than you ever thought you could be!

LET GO!

I want to speak to those whose dreams have shattered, who are bruised and have lost hope for healing to come, to some whose dream for a loved one has been shattered by that person walking away from God, and to others who are bound by compulsive sin but are terrified to let it go, because they fear it is all they have. Let go! Give it to God. Let Him change you, purify you, fulfill you and His plan for your life - His way. Let your dream die that He may RESURRECT it in His will.

To those who are bruised and wounded - let go of your fear! Satan is lying to you telling you that there will be no healing. But David said, "I had fainted unless I had believed to see the goodness of the Lord IN THE LAND OF THE LIVING." (Psalm 27:13) Take hold of His hand. He will not break a bruised reed. He wants to heal your most bitter wound!

Do you have a loved one who has strayed from God? Did God promise their return, yet nothing happened? I believe in intercession. Lift that loved one heavenward and pray! Let go of your human desire to change them. Let go of your human attempts to cause their return to God. As you pray and release them to Him , God will purge you of human efforts to make something happen and give you His heart for that person so you may pray with power.

Are you bound to sin? Satan has lied to you! He has told you that to give up your sin means you will be empty and unfulfilled! God is not a joy-killer who takes sin away and leaves you empty. He only wants to deliver you from the counterfeit and give you the real thing. Every perversion is a counterfeit of something eternally real God wants to give you. You think repentance is a negative thing. It is not! It is merely letting go of the destructive thing and receiving life! You think holiness is a depressing prospect. It is not! Holiness and wholeness are from the same root word. To be holy is to be whole, full of peace, joy and fulfillment! God's "real" will make the counterfeit ugly by comparison. But you must LET GO.

Whatever the dream - nothing is too good to be! A delayed dream is not the end. Ask Joseph. His dream was simply purified, matured and enlarged. God took Joseph's little idea of what God's will was and enlarged Joseph to receive and fulfill that dream. A broken heart is not the end - ask Joseph! Hated by his brothers, abandoned, despairing, he cried out to God. God restored his family. He belonged again! NOTHING is too good to be!

But God had to take time to purge Joseph of bitter things.

A strayed loved one is not the end. Ask Joseph! He was helpless to return his brothers to God. But he prayed, and God answered. Nothing is too good to be!

Are you afraid to let go of some sin you think is filling your emptiness? Are you afraid only emotional loss and sorrow await? It does not! Ask Joseph! Tempted by adultery, he fled, and God found in him a trustworthy man, for Joseph trusted God enough that he wouldn't settle for a cheap counterfeit, and he was fulfilled!

Our Father, eternal Giver, help us to let go. Lift us from despair, help us trust Your delays, yield to Your changes, help us forsake the counterfeits and hold out for the true. Father, You have given us so much. Help us be YOUR dream. May we fulfill Your dream for us.

3 GETTING OUT OF EGYPT

The road to healing is a difficult one. It is strewn with crises, pressure and challenges. Those who haven't traveled this road find it hard to understand those who do. It can be a lonely road. But it is a glorious one, as each step takes you closer to the Father's arms. There are signposts on this road, and I have found the account of the deliverance of the children of Israel has many insights on our personal walk toward holiness and wholeness.

A PLACE OF BONDAGE

Israel, once honored in Egypt, was now in cruel bondage. Satan does not respect second generation religion. Your parents' faith in God will not gain you an ounce of respect with Satan. You must come to Jesus yourself. Bondage will be your future without that personal encounter, no matter what your family's faith.

Moses had it in his heart to see the Israelites free from bondage. But, like us, he attempted to bring that freedom through the flesh. He defended a slave by killing an Egyptian. The next day he was breaking up a fight between two Israelites, and one said, "Are you our ruler? Will you kill us like you did the Egyptian yesterday?" Moses tried to bring deliverance his way, not God's way. Often we do the same. We clamp down on the flesh, condemn ourselves for failure, try to discipline the flesh by denial. We become like those Paul spoke of who lived by the rule, "Touch not. Taste not. Handle not." That is not victory. You cannot discipline or conform the sin nature. It is unredeemable and must be put to death, and that takes a miracle of God. Egypt symbolizes the world and the sin nature, and Moses tried to bring freedom by striking the flesh. He quickly learned 3 lessons. One: Man cannot be set free except for a miracle. "With man it is impossible, but with God, all things are possible." (Mt. 19:26) The sin-nature is too strong to fight. It is unconquerable. Moses knew, as we should, that deliverance cannot come any other way than by God's intervention. Settle it, then. When you are sick enough of the bondage, and your struggle has become desperate and impossible, cry out to God. When you stop trying to battle the flesh, allowing the Spirit of God to take control, He will begin to break the chains of bondage.

Moses' 2nd lesson: Never hurt an Egyptian unless you are prepared to deal with Pharaoh. For Pharaoh learned of the murder and sought to kill

21

Moses. We too must know that when you seek deliverance, and however failingly attempt to be free, Satan's wrath will be loosened, for like a pimp or drug pusher, he will not let go of his victims without a vicious fight. Those seeking deliverance and those interceding on their behalf must know that to pray for freedom whatever it costs is a battle cry which will put you right in the midst of deep and severe warfare.

Moses' 3rd lesson was a surprise: His own people turned on him. "Will you kill us like you did the Egyptian, Moses? Who do you think you are?" He learned that no one rejects like the rejected. No one can inflict hurt like those in pain. Hurt people hurt people. When God begins healing you, those who were bound with you may become vicious and hateful. When Jesus enters the dark corners of our life, do not be surprised that instead of your friends rejoicing, they resent you instead, for your light forces them to decide between receiving the light or rejecting it. Your relationships may change. Anyone who has left a life of chronic drinking with friends understands this: The minute you sober up, you are "no fun anymore" and lose those very "friends" because your relationships were build around a bottle. As healing comes, you will begin to understand that relationships you may have were built on the attraction of mutual sin and spiritual sickness, not on attraction to Christ.

A PLACE OF EXILE

Moses fled Egypt to the wilderness. He felt loneliness and desolation. He had grown up in Egypt, once a powerful man of Egypt. His people were there. He knew nothing BUT Egypt. When God begins to heal you, you will be drawn away from old friends of the world. You may feel exiled. Those who once accepted you now reject you. You cannot go back, but fear what lies ahead. But God calls, "Come away, beloved. Leave the known, that I may show you things you do not know. Leave those you knew, come to know Me."

A PLACE OF DESOLATION

Who really knows how to be healed of hurts? Can anyone give a plan that works for everyone? I believe if we had such a plan, we would miss the point that healing is so we may be in uncontested relationship with Jesus the Lord Jesus. That requires a personal encounter with God. "Lord, You have searched me, and known me." (Ps. 139:11) Personal encounter brings a searching, specific healing work of God that cannot be taught in any book on emotional healing.

A PLACE OF BURNING

"The Lord appeared to him in a flame of fire from the midst of a bush. And the bush burned with fire, but the bush was not consumed." (Ex. 3:2) You may fear healing means giving up what is familiar to you, fear that God will change you into something cold, fearing holiness is confining, empty and lifeless. But our God, a consuming Fire, burns but does not destroy, burning the things that destroy you but not destroying YOU. You don't lose your identity - you find it! I am more "me" than when I first believed, far beyond what I dared believe I could be. Before, sins and sickness were so ingrained that I believed they WERE me, and I feared that if God removed them, there would be no "me" left. To my surprise and joy, I found a childlike, innocent person inside I never knew was there. I'd been purged but not destroyed. What a marvelous discovery! "Love slays what we have been, that we may be what we were not." (Augustine)

A PLACE OF HEALING

As God spoke, Moses was changed. He wasn't forgotten! There was deliverance after all! Recorded there are three of the most powerful words in scripture concerning God's heart: "I have HEARD your cries. I have SEEN your oppression. I KNOW your sorrows." (Ex. 3:7) God sees! God knows! He is not uninvolved! No tear from your eye is forgotten. It is felt in God's very heart. He is not a God afar off! "I will come down and deliver you." He not only knows, but He will come Himself to intervene, not a distant God expecting you to do the best you can, but a God who COMES DOWN to YOU! "I AM THAT I AM." (Ex. 3:14) He is El Shaddai, the all-sufficient one, "I am what you need, all that you need." He is Father and friend. He is YHWH NISSI, our Banner of Defense. He is Comforter and Lord. Tell Him your need, for He is more than enough! He knows even the things you do not know you need, and will fill to overflowing the heart that surrenders to Him.

A PLACE OF CONVERSION

Moses was converted in that encounter. He saw God's glory, and all Egypt's pleasures were forever cheapened and dimmed. Egypt meant nothing to him now, for God had replaced the love of Egypt with the Love of the Eternal God.

We speak mistakenly of conversion as only an unbeliever's experience. Peter, (a believer) was told by Jesus, "I have prayed for you that your faith does not fail, and when you are converted, strengthen your brothers." (Luke

22:32) Convert means to return, to twist around. If Peter, as a believer, needed conversion, so do we! The place of desolation can be the place of conversion, away from distraction and the things of the world, an encounter with the Living God. Each stage in my healing has come through dryness; desperation, desolation and then revelation of Jesus in my heart. That is why to teach the HOW of healing without the WHO is pointless, for healing is to replace darkness with the Light of the World, replace the world with Jesus Himself. If this does not happen, then it is not the true healing of God. When He reveals Himself in our hour of pain, our word becomes, "I have heard of You by the hearing of the ear, but now my eye sees You." (Job 42:5) We no longer know merely about Him; We know HIM. All that went before becomes tasteless. You reach Jordan, and in crossing it, you know there is nothing to go back to, you must go on, cost what it may.

PRESSURE AND CONFRONTATION

Moses returned with a message to Pharaoh: LET MY PEOPLE GO! Pharaoh responded by taking away the very straw Hebrew slaves were to make bricks with, and they became bitter and blamed Moses. It is critical that both intercessors and those seeking deliverance know that Satan viciously holds the bound. God will give a word of deliverance; but you must know, that word is the drawing of a battle line for that life. After receiving such a word, you may be met with worsening conditions and pressures, and you may be tempted to cry, "God, why have you forsaken me?" But after the promise will come the pressure and the battle. Prepare to lock horns in holy anger against the very forces of hell! "But why doesn't God just deliver me NOW?" Because He intends to strengthen your faith, allowing a great contest in which your victory is certain and glorious! If it were an instant deliverance, you might quickly take it for granted, bypassing the growth potential and maturity that comes in battle. I've seen those claiming instant deliverance, and they may be released from outward sins, but they STILL will have to let God dig out the roots! God desires to raise in you a strong child, a valiant warrior. Do not fight the process, or despair at the pressure, for it will bring real deliverance, and genuine healing that is stable, mature and permanent.

The rest we know. God sent many great judgments on Egypt before Pharaoh let Israel go. But as surely as He promised, great deliverance came. Bondage behind them, they joyfully set out for the blessed land of inheritance.

TREASURE

Not only was freedom released, but they left with great wealth and treasure from the Egyptians. I have a word for all who look to the Land of Promise by faith: You shall come from your bondage with great wealth! "I will rebuild Jerusalem on her ruins." He doesn't throw away the mistakes; He uses them! Even the greatest failures and sins are not without profit for the child of God. Even in failure, there will not only be deliverance, but great wealth from the very things you thought loss. No matter how shameful your past, how great your wounds, let God cause you to look back fearlessly, fully forgiven, to find that treasure. Nothing for the believer is wasted. There are insights to retrieve, lessons to establish, great treasure to be gained, wisdom that will smooth the path before you and strengthen the hand of those who are yet to inherit the great miracle of His healing hand.

4 SUFFERING

Much has been written about suffering, yet more needs to be said. Some believe suffering is always God's will - some believe it is never, and many are just confused and in pain. Perhaps the following insights will help.

There are several Bible words for suffering: Experience, enclose, besiege, render infamous, hold up against, roof over, cover with silence, pursue, deficit. These words tell me that the value or worthlessness of a trial depends on our posture. Suffering should never be accepted in defeat or spiritual passivity. You STAND and ENDURE and BATTLE until there is RELEASE. Battle? Of course. I believe the answer that was given to Paul in his trial of "my grace is sufficient"- though His grace always IS enough - is the exception, not the rule.

We must resolve some things about suffering. First, it is never the ideal, but a neutral reality that God can use, but make no mistake, suffering was NEVER God's intention for His creation in the beginning. It is a FACT OF LIFE. Recognize that suffering is a result of the fall, sin, man's failure, and not divinely authored pain to keep us in line and keep God happy. God is not the author of suffering. If you believe He is, then maybe you've got a bad surprise waiting for you in heaven - MORE SUFFERING! Thank God, no! Suffering is merely a fact, a bad reality that God will use and give us the power to overcome if we let Him.

Interestingly, the word suffering is used about 28 times in reference to persecution for the Gospel and the Word of God. I doubt many of us know what that means! Several references are to suffering for others, several for our own sins and several more in identification with Christ's own heart. Most references dealt with Satanic opposition through others because you're standing in Christ.

So how do we view suffering? First, discern the source. I'm deeply concerned with many Christians who live in defeat because Satan has attacked and they automatically assume it is God's will to remain in pain! I especially think of those who were born into suffering and torment and have lived with constant emotional abuse and pain. It is one thing to accept suffering, opposition and attack as a result of your testimony and threat to Satan's dominion, but quite another to accept unresolved, destructive, tormenting fruitless pain without a question and a fight. You may bring up Paul's thorn in the flesh. Please note that Paul did not automatically accept

27

the thorn. He besought the Lord to remove it three times before God gave him a special word and grace to endure it. His first posture was a fighting posture. Just as it is wrong to believe a Christian need never suffer, it is

equally wrong to believe that's all there is. We need a balance. God told us He has given us all things richly to enjoy. (1 Tim. 6:17) If your life is all torment and no enjoyment and blessing, I urge you to examine the source of the pain. It may be that you have been victimized by the lie that to serve Christ is to suffer torment until you die.

When the average person speaks of suffering, they mean discomfort, pressure, struggle in growth, etc. This seems to be the general scriptural description of much trial. But some people, and these are the ones I so long to comfort, have known nothing but daily torment, and Satan lies and tells them this is NORMAL CHRISTIAN SUFFERING! Please understand this critical word: Torment is NEVER, EVER of God for the believer. For example, one man I know, because of devastating emotional wounds, Satanic pressures and deep destruction, was overwhelmed by sexual compulsion. He was told his torment was "normal temptation." No wonder he was defeated! What kind of a God would allow His child to suffer agonizing torture to sin and fail? This same man, after God began to heal the wounds and deliver him from Satanic bondage, recently experienced his first REAL temptation, and he was ecstatic! It wasn't a driving, uncontrollable torment, but a manageable, clearly seen outside pressure, not an inside nightmare! What a difference! And how it changed his heart toward God to know God did not author or desire him to suffer such unbearable pain.

How do we know normal trial from Satanic attack? We must know Satan's voice. He torments. He then comes disguised as God, playing on our own hurt-developed conception of God: "You talk too much. You lust. You drink. Look how messed up you are! I'm punishing you for sinning last year. I can't bless you when you're such a mess. Straighten up! You don't pray enough. You don't study the Bible. Go to church! That's your problem! You don't go to church and you're a mess! Why don't you witness? You're such a lousy Christian." This is how we recognize the Tormentor: He always accuses, and he's never specific, and he brings up things that have already been put under the blood of Jesus. If we buy it, we accept tragedy and torment as punishment, or we'll go back to the law, thinking that God will stop tormenting us if we just stop doing this and that.

But God does not condemn, and He speaks SPECIFICALLY. Satan just comes and says, "This is your lot in life. Just accept it." God doesn't do that! God will be specific if our suffering is a result of a hurt needing healing, or being sinned against, or because of Satanic opposition. But know this: He will always give you an answer, or a way out, or a battle plan, or a great, overwhelming peace and grace to endure. If there is no answer, no grace, no peace and no letup, you may do well to rip off the mask and see the God-imitator Satan beneath it!

It is common for us to believe we are being punished for sins when we suffer. Too many of us reinforce that notion! Even the disciples were guilty: "Lord, who sinned, this man or his parents, that he was born blind?" "Neither," Jesus replied, "But that the works of God may be manifest in him." (John 9:3) But perhaps you say, you HAVE sinned against God. And you are suffering for it. But sin has a natural consequence. God does not send it! "The backslider shall be filled with his own ways. " (Pr. 14:14) "Your own backslidings shall reprove you." (Jer. 2:19) God doesn't punish you when you've sought forgiveness. If a little boy disobeys and burns his hand on a stove, no other punishment is needed and no normal parent would add beating to a third degree burn. Jesus is your friend and advocate, your defender, not your enemy.

God does discipline, but many are so filled with self-hatred that we mistake bloody abuse from Satan for discipline from God. Never! Jesus spoke of the Heavenly Father being much more than earthly ones. So let me give a fit analogy: show me a parent that enjoys seeing their child suffer, and I'll show you a sick person. (Lam. 3:33)

"But what about the fellowship of His sufferings?" (Philippians 3:10) But God didn't torment Jesus, people did. Satan did. He resisted Satan and loved the abusers - so what are His sufferings? We know He is ascended, so he is not sick and Satan can't torment him. His present sufferings are rejection, heartache for the lost and hurt for His bruised and rebellious people. And if you are Christ-centered, these will be your sufferings as well. That is not torment but an acceptable offering to God - identifying with His own pain.

Our attitude toward suffering is the issue. Just as our message is not, "Come to Jesus and your problems are over," neither is it "Come to Jesus and be miserable." Jesus didn't come to torment people, but to set them free. He healed the sick, delivered the oppressed, brought hope to the downcast. It's not a message of bad news, but good news! It's not just when we go to heaven, either. David said, "I had fainted unless I had believed to see the goodness of the Lord IN THE LAND OF THE LIVING." (Ps. 27:13) Jesus came to bring that goodness to us. Paul learned, yes, to be abased but also to abound. For some it's easier to accept abasement because it is all they have known, and they feel it is all they deserve. But God wants to meet, not frustrate your heart's needs. Yes, man doesn't live by bread alone, but he doesn't live by spirit alone either. The Pharisees were all spiritual. The people hated them because they didn't care for those in need. Jesus came to meet those needs, to fill them. Do we have that Gospel? Or is ours a glum-faced, "Turn or burn, come to Jesus and be empty" attitude? Jesus healed, fed, comforted and set free, and offered fullness of life. Trouble-free? Of course not: "In the world ye shall have tribulation." But it is not all pain. "Be of good cheer! I have overcome the world!" In all trial, He is our friend, our advocate, helping us to conquer, change, assault and stand.

I do not pretend there are always answers for suffering. But I do believe our first posture when we see one suffer is to get the mind of God as to its source, and do all we can by the power of God to MEET THAT NEED. We should seek to relieve the suffering one. THAT is God's will. Comfort the broken. Heal the sick. Release the captives.

Do not feel because you are suffering that you are targeted by God. Seek to know the source and the reason. If it is pain resulting from inner wounds, God wants to heal it! If it is suffering at others' hands, God wants to give you victory over it. If it is Satanic, God wants you to do battle with it until it yields in total defeat. Never assume it's because you're doing something wrong. Satan is trying to put out all the lightbulbs he can in this hour. Neither be closed to the fact that perhaps God IS trying to tell you to change something that has become a source of suffering.

One thing you must do. If you are suffering, storm God's gates until something gives. It may be an answer as to how to fight, what to change, or what needs healing. Or it may be a time of trial for growth. But if there is no answer, no letup and no peace, then I can tell you for sure it is not any part of God. If all suffering produces is hardness, bitterness and defeat, it is not of God at all.

One final matter. 1 Peter says, "The God of all peace, after you have suffered a little while, (literally, "puny time-span") strengthen, establish, settle you." (I Pet, 5:10) Suffering is only *part* of our growth experience. I'm convinced we must grow as much through blessing as adversity. If you don't have this balance, I believe God longs to give you much, much more. Expect it! Ask for it! "You have not because you ask not." Suffering is never the full-time lot for the Christian. It wasn't for Job, and it is not for us. God is your Loving Father. Discipline is only a part. Resist what you can, endure what you must and always know God is neither the tormentor nor the author thereof. He allows trial at times for growth. But there's no suffering in heaven, and no one can convince me He doesn't want us to experience a balance of that now. Trial may come, but it is not our career: "Many are the afflictions of the righteous, but the Lord delivers them out of them ALL." (Ps, 34:19)

Gregory R Reid

5 THE HEART OF TRUE MINISTRY

The closer we come to the heart of our Beloved, the more we will be motivated to true ministry. It will mean radical changes in our understanding of what ministry is. Ministry is simply the love and compassion of Jesus extended through His people. Just as Satan and demons must have a body to live in and destroy through, so God seeks a body He can love and heal through.

The center of true ministry is our fellowship with Jesus. If our love relationship with Him is not of first importance, we will either try to do something for God out of fleshly zeal, or we will do nothing at all. But it is impossible to share intimately with Jesus without being moved by the things that move Him.

Since the fall, God's heart has cried out to restore man to that fellowship of love with Himself. The scriptures are filled with that longing of God. And there is another cry of God throughout scripture: "Who will go for us?" (Is. 6:8) and, "I sought for a man to stand in the gap..." (Ez.22:30) God has found only a few. Why?

It is costly. I once read a book entitled, "Let my heart be broken by the things that break the heart of God." To move into true ministry, you must come close enough to the heart of the Beloved to allow your heart to be broken, to share His burden for the lost and wounded. Few of us want to pay that price. I'm afraid we've made ministry far too glamorous - results, finances, recognition. We've made it a career, a side-line, a "job". But I'm convinced that ministry that pays more than it costs is at best shallow and temporal. History is too full of saints that died of broken hearts for the lost for us to take ministry lightly. IT WILL COST OUR LIVES! True ministry comes through lives which have been tested by that which they now speak of, whose outflow of love and power comes from hearts that are intimately bound to the heart of Jesus. They do not divorce ministry from family, jobs, friends or even leisure. All of life becomes an opportunity to share Jesus with others. And isn't that what ministry is really all about? Ministry is Jesus the person, alive and longing to bring people into wholeness and power.

Why has healing power gone out of much of our preaching? Jesus said, "What I tell you in secret, that shout from the housetops." You can't shout something you haven't received. Our secret place of intimacy with Jesus has been lost, and we can only repeat yesterday's teaching, because we

33

haven't taken the time to come to Him for a fresh understanding of His Word. If we long to bring manna to the hungry, we have to stay close enough to Jesus to receive it from Him.

Yesterday's word, movement or revelation will not suffice anymore. It would be good for us to remember that the Apostles had no sermon files or audio libraries to draw from. They were simply filled with the love and power of God, and "the people took knowledge of them, that they had been with Jesus." (Acts 4:13)

Ministry comes from those willing to agonize before God on man's behalf, and plead before man on God's behalf. How many tears have we shed for broken lives? But more, how many tears have we shed in the grief of God for mankind?

I also believe we've become too far removed from the world. We're cloistered. We're out of touch with the needs of the broken. We prefer to "let them come to us." I believe that the more believers who come closely to Jesus' heart, the more they will find themselves out where people are. Fellowship among us should be a filling station, not a permanent retreat. It is where we are strengthened in the battle, it is not a permanent leave to keep us off the front lines. I'm afraid we as the church have simply lost our relevance. People listened to Jesus because He related to people in and concerning their own environment and surroundings. He understood their needs, and was not afraid of their sins. The Pharisees, those great knowledge-dispensers and law keepers, were totally separated and unconcerned for people, and they resented Jesus because He spoke to people's hearts, and with authority. He did not separate himself from the crowds and sinners. He knew that in being among them, He could touch them, and He was not afraid to be touched *by* them. Oh, friends, we act so shocked by the world and its ways, we are so afraid of sinners! How can we ever expect to reach the lost if we're not willing to go to them with the love of God, where they are at, just as they are? I was greatly moved by an interview with Floyd McClung of YWAM. He had moved his family to the heart of the brothels in Amsterdam. The interviewer, a little shocked, said, "Well, how do you reach the prostitutes? You obviously don't go into the brothels." "Yes, we do," he replied. "We go in and talk to them and ask if we can pray for them." Taken aback, the interviewer asked, "Then how do you hate their sin while still loving the sinner?" McClung simply replied, "We just love them. We are their friends."

This man understands God's heart toward the lost! McClung once said, "People don't care how much you know until they know how much

34

you care." I believe that with all my heart.

Jesus is looking for a passionate people. We've become so knowledge oriented, we've lost our heart. Jesus was PASSIONATE. In ANGER He overthrew the moneychangers. He WEPT over Jerusalem. He leapt with JOY and He DANCED because the disciples understood truth. Do you understand? Ours has become a heartless Gospel. We know all the truth but our hearts are not in it. New believers are so precious! They are in love with Jesus, and there we are, waiting in the wings for them to "settle down" so we can make them lifeless like us. Now I just want to take these new babes and say, "Never lose your fire. Love Jesus. Love Him with all you've got, and don't ever let anyone rob you of that passion." I truly believe people don't listen to us because they know we're just reciting things that are no longer alive and vital to us. The Apostles, on the other hand, were a different breed. They were passionate people. The touch of Jesus' love put a fire in them that created intense love, joy and fervor. They were expressing HIS heart. What a contrast that is to all our formula-oriented ministry and projects "for God"! Show me a person who has experienced brokenness over people's needs, who is full of love and compassion, to whom knowing Jesus' heart has become everything, and I'11 show you a living definition of Jesus' ministry.

There is a difference between shepherds and hirelings. A hireling is paid to do a job. He might as well be working for AT&T. He's conveniently distanced from people. They are there for his benefit. Ministry is just a job. (Often a well-paying one!) But you cannot pay a true shepherd enough to stay OUT of serving God's people! He would PAY to serve (and he does in many ways) for it burns in him like a fire. I weep as I see pastors and ministry leaders who are so removed from the hurting people of the church and the world that they are ministering death and words without power. I have only met a few true shepherds - heart-servants - and they were people whose very lives emanated a certain wounding of God that produced depth, and power, and love. It cost them something to be His heart! It cost them something to be able to pour out of His love. It is strange that what I recall most about these lovers of God was not their words but the spirit of love and power they stood in, and it has made me understand that 100 scriptures through someone who has not been broken by God's broken heart will do little...one verse through one touched by His heart can bring healing and life.

Yes, it costs something to touch true ministry. I know God begins with many of us on the basis of our zeal. But we must go beyond zeal. Moses did something "for God" - he killed a man and spent 40 years in exile. But I believe he came into true ministry when he said, "God, if You don't spare these people, blot MY name out of Your book!" And Paul, who wrote, "Woe to me if I do not preach," later said, "I wish I could be damned from Christ if my brethren could be saved." Incredible! They loved so deeply that they would lay down their lives for another's salvation. Do you understand?

Do you know what it is to weep until your gut hurts because someone is lost? Have you spent even one sleepless night in prayer over a broken life? Anyone can dispense answers. But power comes from truth that comes from your heart, your gut, your LIFE. If spending one hour listening to someone wearies you, do something besides serve. If someone's tears and agony make you uncomfortable, you may be in the wrong profession. For if you really desire to be His vessel of love, He will put you right in the dirt and mire, the blood and guts of human need. For love always seeks the lowest, deepest level of need. He'll call you from ivory palaces and put you among the homeless. The call is still going forth: "Who will go for Us?" You don't need a degree in theology. You just need a willing heart. All you need is to draw close to the Beloved, to share His burdens, to respond *with* Him to others. True ministry is walking *with* Jesus through humanity, allowing Him to touch and heal through your yielded heart. For love's nature must give...must heal...must love. It is more than recognition, success or anything else we've come to call "the ministry". It is a divine compulsion. Paul summed up the heart of it all: "The love of Christ compels us." Love is the only true motive for ministry - Jesus' ministry. Lord, grant us that compulsion!

6 BITTERNESS

There are two kinds of believers: the strong and able, and the weak and wounded. Satan knows how to paralyze the one and destroy the other. He takes the strong and able and makes them relatively useless by making them apathetic toward the mandate of sharing Jesus, and addicting them to worldly security and self-sufficiency, They are saved, they love God, but their self-strength has become their trap. Thank God, there are those God has blessed with abundant provision and strength, and they know it is a gift to be used to help those in need.

I want to address this to the others - the weak and wounded. This is how Satan works: First, he engineers a number of encounters with insensitive or loveless Christians. At a point when a wounded believer becomes desperate enough to trust someone and be vulnerable about their struggles or need for deliverance or love, they experience rejection, misunderstanding and abuse. As I've said before, it is wrong to use the excuse of "we're only human" when we hurt people, because our humanity, Spirit-filled, is the very tool God uses to love through - human arms, hands and hearts yielded to the love of God.

Second, Satan renders the person so wounded that they can't see through the pain of rejection and can't see Jesus in their hour of need. The scriptures say we, who are strong, ought to bear the infirmities of the weak. If we who are strong and can (if we choose) love, can (if we choose) give, be compassionate, and bring healing don't do so, we've broken a commandment of love, and worse, we've crippled another's ability to see Jesus and receive His Love.

The last and often fatal attack on the now alienated and bleeding believer is bitterness. It is to this I want to speak. It is the Jordan where the wounded either pass over in faith or draw back in fear and die. I've spoken of the need for the strong to love and bring healing to others. But the strong change slowly, usually only in crisis, and the wounded can't wait for the change. So I am writing to you who have been injured. These will be hard words but it will be a lifeline if you receive what I say.

NO EXCUSE

Rejection by Christians is no excuse for bitterness! Few have seen the lack of love in the church as I have witnessed, and I understand the reason you may be bitter - but if you give way to bitterness, it will surely destroy you. Over the years, I've met dozens of people who once served the Lord but were hurt, became bitter and turned away from believers altogether. They became alcoholics, drug abusers, their marriages fell apart, or they became sexually promiscuous. They are merely shells. They will tell you about hurts that happened 30 years ago, just like it was yesterday. Others set themselves up as judges of the church, telling you of all their hurts and encouraging you to take on an "I don't need Christians" attitude like them. They have an air of authority and self-specialness, even believing they are "called" to expose Christians and draw young believers into their corner.

MARKS OF BITTERNESS

The mark of bitterness comes out of the mouth, for "out of the abundance of the heart the mouth speaks." Bitter people are negative, cynical, sarcastic and self-pitying. They remember and recite in bitter detail every incident where a Christian failed them.

Are you relating to this? I do, for I waged a terrible war with my own bitterness. From the time I came to the Lord, I experienced repeated hurts and rejection from Christians, and I accumulated each one, becoming more angry and bitter with each new hurt. My time of confrontation came at Bible School through a couple who were like parents to me. In the beginning, we had some healthy exchange of emotions about the lack of love among believers. But for me, it became the center of our fellowship - a place to vent my bitterness.

Five minutes after I had arrived at their apartment one day, the husband went to his bedroom. I thought he was on the phone. I continued my tirades while his wife quietly washed dishes. I finally said, "Where's Dave?" She said, "He's hiding out. He can't stand your bitterness anymore." (Long pause) "Neither can I." It was like a knife. I left, got angry, convinced myself they were just like all the others! Slowly, it hit me - I was so vile and bitter that I was turning my own friends away. Oh, it HURT to admit - I was the problem! Now I understood what Paul said: "Looking diligently lest anyone fall short of the grace of God; lest any root of bitterness springing up cause trouble, and by this many are defiled." (Heb. 12:15) I was bringing uncleanness to others by my bitter mouth. Nothing but hurt and destruction came from my mouth.

I went for counseling with the school administrator who I greatly respected for his compassion and insight. He listened patiently to my bitter words and hurt. I don't remember all he said. But when he prayed for me, my head hurt - I became dizzy and almost passed out - then, like a dark cloud, something lifted from me, a dark and oppressive force. Bitterness had opened the door to demonic oppression that literally fed my thoughts and words. I was delivered that day.

The real battle with bitterness began from there. There were more hurts. I had to start reprogramming my thoughts and words. I took David's psalm as my daily prayer: "Set a guard, O Lord, over my mouth; keep watch over the door of my lips." I had to force myself to leave conversations with bitter people. The bitterness was slowly uprooted. But I could never let my guard down again. The ROOT of bitterness (which lies in our old nature) is always there. I must be sure it has no fertile ground in my heart.

I've heard from so many wounded Christians, "Christians are phony and uncaring. I get more fellowship at the bars!" I know Christians can be terribly unloving. But hear me: It is a fatal error to exchange fellowship with believers for fellowship with the world! The Christian family isn't a club. "They didn't like me so I'll go to people that do." With all its unlove and flaws, Christians are of the same blood. Christ-centered fellowship (and I recognize how rare that is among us) is an exchange of life - a mysterious spiritual connection which produces life. There is another dynamic, no less real, in the fellowship of unbelievers. They are in darkness. They exchange death to each other. They are slaves to death and darkness, as we are children of light. They may be friendly, accepting and kind, but darkness still owns them. Paul said, "Don't be unequally yoked with unbelievers; For what fellowship has righteousness with lawlessness, or what communion has light with darkness?" (2 Cor. 6:14) By nature we are different. Granted, some unbelievers act better than believers, and some very religious Christians can act like the devil himself. It doesn't matter. Being a Christian isn't a way of ACTING, it is an IDENTITY. Fellowship means to link as a chain. Of course we befriend and care for unbelievers to lead them to Jesus. But if in bitterness to believers you link with unbelievers, you will begin to assimilate their actions, ideology and way of life. You deny your identity and become subject to the forces of darkness. In your hurt, if you turn to the world for comfort and fellowship, Satan will open the door and it will be a deadly trap. It hurts to see so many of my friends who were wounded become bitter and turn to the world, because the road back is a long, painful one.

Perhaps you've been hurt, and you're afraid to give Christians another chance. Beloved friend, you must take a bold step of maturity. Healing comes when you stop feeling sorry for yourself. Don't you realize there are others who are also being hurt? Who will help them? Who can better understand their needs and hurts besides YOU? Bitter people only think, "I wasn't loved." Overcomers say, "Who can I love?" Bitter people think, "The church never helped me." Overcomers say, "Who can I help?" You may see all the flaws of the church well. You have a choice to make: Stay bitter, or turn your heart to God and be different! BE the kind of believer who IS sensitive and caring!

Bitterness enables you to blame everyone and everything for your inability to serve Jesus. Bitterness can make you into a Saul who blamed David, his son, the people - but never brokenly took responsibility for his response to hurt before God.

Many others in scripture had reasons for bitterness but instead became more loving, forgiving people. Perhaps Joseph of the Old Testament had the most reasons to be bitter. He was betrayed by his brothers, he barely avoided them murdering him, only to be sold into slavery. Promoted out of prison, he was betrayed because he stayed true to God and was sent back to prison. He was promised by a King's prisoner he had helped that he would be freed, only to be forgotten and forsaken again. Bitterness? Friend, you don't even begin to understand bitter circumstances until you understand Joseph. But because Joseph trusted God and refused to be bitter, God restored to him all things.

Now we come to the key. Joseph left us with one statement that can destroy your bitterness and change your life, if you make it your own: "But as for you, you meant evil against me, BUT GOD MEANT IT FOR GOOD." (Gen. 50:20) If you are ready to deal bitterness a death blow, here is your key to deliverance: Write down every hurt and bitter feeling you have, from every person, every hate and unforgiveness. Take it to God and say, "I forgive them." Then look again at the faces, people and circumstances you've written and say aloud, "What Satan intended for evil, God means it for good!" Then torch it. Burn it. LET IT GO! Yes, you'll still battle. When bitter feelings or anger resurface over old wounds, then you must raise up the truth of Romans 8:28: God is at work in ALL THINGS to produce good! ALL things! Every hurt and rejection, God will work through them to produce good in you.

Stop hanging with bitter people. It has been rightly said that the most vicious, divisive Christians are those wounded by churches but who never deal with their bitterness. Set a guard at your lips.

And if someone hurts you, you will have reached maturity when you refuse to hide behind the petty and cowardly wall of gossip and you will step forward to confront the offender, which is your right and responsibility according to scripture.

Before you, dear one, is a door. Have the guts to deal bitterness a death blow before it deals it to you. Dare to believe God can make good of the evil, to make you strong, loving and compassionate. Don't take the path back to the world - stand for what you know is true, even if it is a lonely path. Dare to believe there really ARE believers who care - and be willing to win this battle for the sake of others who will need you.

Gregory R Reid

7 THRESHING

We have to learn to handle people God's way. I've read many Christian counseling books. Some are very cut and dry, advising counselors to just state the scriptural facts and demand that the person follow through or sever the counseling sessions. Others are more liberal, using situational ethics and bending the scriptures. I'd like to offer another way.

We have to recognize that people are complex and each person has their own history. When I first began counseling, I had my dozen or so scriptural remedies, and no matter what the situation, I dispensed them like pills and if it didn't work for the person, it was obvious to me that they weren't right with God. But the more I studied scripture, and the more I counseled, the more I realized that the Bible is deeper and broader than my own pat answers, and only the Holy Spirit knew what the person needed. I've met with some people who are so damaged that there are *several* major areas of sin needing to be dealt with. What do I deal with first? How do I approach it scripturally? I knew one man who was bound by homosexuality, pornography, alcohol and occult practices. In my own wisdom, I felt homosexuality was the first thing to confront. The Holy Spirit said no; the occult practices had to be dealt with first. With another person, perhaps they are having problems with internet pornography. Of course it is sin. But as they forsake it, it will make it easier to stick with the commitment if the Holy Spirit moves the person into strong fellowship first, because He knows that fellowship will give the person the spiritual strength they need to overcome their temptations.

In other words, to be effective counselors we have to let the Holy Spirit be the Counselor. That's His Name, that is His work. We fail because we have formulas for every sin and hurt. We end up playing God over someone's life.

I recently was reminded of a verse that helped me to understand that work of Jesus: "He doesn't thresh all grains the same." (Isaiah 28:28a Living Bible) Have you ever wondered why some people seem to be continually chastised by the Lord, while others don't ever seem to struggle very much? Well, God doesn't thresh all grains the same. He alone knows what we need. The threshing of God is to take the chaff away and produce fruit in us and through us. Some grains have to be threshed gently, because they are soft and easily damaged. Others have very hard encasements and must be handled more roughly. God alone knows which we are, and that is why we can't "assume" what a person needs to hear or do.

Some time ago, I was in one of the most painful times of my Christian life. I was broke, homeless, almost friendless. I was hurting and desperate. A friend came to me and said, "God is in this. He knows because of your background, wounds, sins and problems that the only way He can ever free you is by harshly dealing with you. Otherwise, you would destroy yourself." That's the last thing I wanted to hear! I was already in enough pain, I didn't ask for the horrible events of my childhood, it was UNFAIR! But now I understand. I was so bound by self-deception and pride that God had to raze my life to the foundation in order to rebuild me. Because He loved me! I wouldn't change one iota of those dealings of God, because it produced a peace and stability in me I would have never had, if I had refused His hand.

Others don't seem to go through much at all! How I used to resent that. They prospered, they had friends and good jobs and families. When God did deal with them, it was seemingly gently and not very earth-shaking. Now I understand; some of those sweet folks don't have the emotional or physical constitution to handle much pain, and they may have a solid upbringing that doesn't necessitate a severe dealing of God. He threshes all grains differently!

Regarding scriptures and counseling, it is so important not to run roughshod over people with our quick verses. I firmly believe that the Bible is the infallible Word of God. It can't be changed. That doesn't give me the right, however, to pick a few scriptures regarding sin and throw them at someone just because of what I see outwardly. I may see someone who outwardly is an alcoholic, and I'll want to quote all the scriptures on drunkenness. (Odds are the person already knows they are sinning.) The Holy Spirit may see inside and know that this person lost his wife in an auto accident, and he desperately needs to deal with and be healed of his grief before he can overcome his problem. Do you understand?

Someone may accuse me of preaching situational ethics. I'm not. But I'll make it clear that while I'm conservative in theology, I am liberal in application. You may say, "But the Bible is clear about sin. We have to confront people and make them forsake their sins." First, only occasionally do people need to be told they are sinning. They know it. Second, the scriptures cover hundreds of sins, from adultery to gluttony, from murder to gossip. Isn't it interesting that we always go for the "big sins," and tend to ignore the "lesser sins"? I heard from a friend about a holiness revival years ago. Brother Brown was preaching a hellfire sermon on holiness, and he went up to Sister Smith on the front row who smoked like a chimney.

He pointed in her face and said, "What are you going to use for an ashtray in heaven, Sister?" She thought for a moment and said, "Well, I think maybe I'll just use your coffee cup." (Not that I am saying coffee is sinful. No, never. It's just an illustration...) The point is that Brother Brown has his own pet sins he doesn't like and hammered people on, and he tends to those in his own life. That is why it is so important in counseling to first ask God to finger anything in YOUR life that is wrong, THEN ask the Holy Spirit to help you deal with the other person. And never forget that our natural tendency is to look only at the outward; the scriptures say not to judge by outward appearance, but on the heart.

This is the crux, really, of ministering to people by His Spirit; God is much less concerned with actions than He is the things in the heart.. Attitudes. Motives. Did you know that two people can commit the same sin with different motives? Proverbs 6 says that a man who takes another man's wife (stealing) will get wounds and dishonor. Yet a thief will not be despised if he steals food because he's HUNGRY. One stole from greed. One from need. Both were sin; both necessitated payment; but the one who stole from need was much less harshly dealt with. The intent and motive of the heart is what God judges. Don't ever judge an action until you understand the intent. Some people commit what we call "small" sins, like gossip, and are never called into account, when they need strong rebuke. Others may commit what we think of as "greater" sins, yet God may want to handle them more gently that we, because He knows the desperation of their hearts. I'm not going soft on sin. ALL sin is serious and to be dealt with; but GOD'S way, in HIS time and with HIS HEART.

I think the Pharisees were much like some of our modern Christian counselors. They knew the law and expected everyone to live up to it like they did. They expected that the coming Messiah would do the same. Instead, He came in mercy. He confirmed the law. He upheld it. But He understood the inability of man to do it without Him. And while upholding the reality of sin, the law and judgment, He extended the most mercy to those deepest in sin, because He saw their hearts and their helplessness. He knew why they did what they did. It's interesting to me that when we talk about the woman caught in adultery, we are so quick to say, "Sure, Jesus said, 'Neither do I condemn you,' but He also said, 'Go and sin no more.'" How vital it is to understand that the power to "go and sin no more" only becomes real when we hear, "I do not condemn you"!

Again, God isn't looking so much at action as motive. You see, the Pharisees didn't *do* any bad things; they were simply rotten in the heart. Jesus saw that and condemned them with vehemence. There are many other instances in scripture to illustrate this. Jacob was a liar and a con artist. His brother was a good guy, but he despised his spiritual heritage. God saw that Jacob, although he was doing wrong, could be spiritually changed. Esau didn't do any great sin, but his heart was hard to the things of God. If we were there, we might have disfellowshipped Jacob and put Esau on our pulpit committee! Or, David and Saul. David was a murderer, adulterer. He was punished, but he never lost his throne because God said he was a man following God's heart. Saul only did *little* things! But those little things were monsters to God, like pride, self-pity and envy. He lost it all because his heart motive became totally impure.

We can uphold the truth of God's Word without playing God in the way we apply it to people. Only the Spirit knows the heart. Only He knows how to thresh; only He knows what a person needs, and we must LISTEN and let the Spirit tell us what to do. Let our word be: Let mercy triumph over judgment; let the Word of Truth stand unchanged; look to the heart before judging the action; and never forget that the Holy Spirit is the only true counselor. We are just His vessels.

8 THE OTHER SIDE OF GRACE

We only seem to think of grace in relation to forgiveness of sins. We sin and say, "Thank God for grace." And we should. Some only use grace and never change their way of life. Forgiveness is the first step, a foundation, but to stop there is to render grace ineffective to change your life. What is the grace of God really for?

GRACE IS THE POWER TO OVERCOME

God never intended grace to just be an "out" or intended us to remain bound by sin. "For sin shall not have dominion over you, for you are not under law, but under grace." The scriptures tell us the strength of sin is the law. To me it's clear that the system of law never brought redemption but condemnation as it brought out man's rebellion, showing his hopeless condition for what it was. That means grace was meant to do what the law couldn't - free us from the power of sin! "Sin shall not have dominion over you" is not an unattainable reality. We remain chained, sometimes because we don't really want to be free, but most often because we have only received grace for salvation and not the immense power of grace to deliver us from sin's chains.

What keeps us from this kind of grace? Pride. "I can handle it." And we never become desperate enough to understand our helplessness. If we "handle" it, God won't. We grossly underestimate the overwhelming power of sin and our helplessness over it. Self-help, self-improvement theology is band-aid theology against the evil of sin.

Growing up, I was saddled with bondages that were unmoveable and consuming. I tried therapy, self-help books, will power - all utterly useless. I came to the cross defeated, totally unable to help myself. "Nothing in my hands I bring...simply to Thy cross I cling." In coming to the end of myself, God poured out grace - power! One by one, impossible bondages were rendered powerless! Each succeeding bondage was defeated the same way - desperation which brought me to emptiness and the cross. Most people never conquer besetting little closet sins because they never get desperate enough to receive the power of grace to change. Grace much more abounds where sin abounds because deep sin shatters the illusion of self-sufficiency.

God's absolute desire is that "those who receive abundance of grace and of the gift of righteousness will reign in life through Jesus Christ." (Ro. 5:17) The reason we don't reign in this life is that we've received grace for salvation but have not received ABUNDANCE of grace. It's part of our upbringing: "God helps those who help themselves." But Jesus said, "Without Me you can do nothing." We're powerless because we do *plenty* without Him. When things get tough, we may ask God for strength - but never understand that He IS our strength. A Spirit-filled walk of resurrection power means you understand 24 hour a day absolute dependence on Christ. We don't like that! We want to do it ourselves because it builds our pride. "Now to him who works, the wages are not counted as grace, but as debt." We bargain with God. "I'll give you $10, and I am expecting a 100 fold return." But grace is a lifelong understanding that we DESERVE nothing, we can earn nothing, and in so coming naked to the cross, we receive EVERYTHING we need.

GRACE & PRIDE

I'm so torn by seeing us like self-sufficient little gods, calling on Him only when it's convenient. No wonder we're ineffective. The scriptures are full of people who came to the end of their self-sufficiency and found transformation. The measure of grace we receive is contingent on one question: Is Christ PART of your life - or IS He your life? Is He?

Pride is the #1 grace-killer we as the church must face. "Come see the astounding miracle crusade..." "This is the most important ministry on the earth!" "God has anointed ME to take the gospel to all the world!" Oh, friends, how can we walk in grace when we're so self-important? Isn't it telling that you never hear a TV or radio evangelist say, "God has called me to a small, neighborhood ministry"? Why is it always, "If you send This Ministry a gift, God will prosper you," why do you never hear someone say, "Don't send money to us, buy a poor family down the street some groceries. You may not get your money back, but you sure will make God happy." We're not walking in grace, for grace and self-importance cannot dwell together. We build, we increase, but WHY? A recent national rally had as its objective to, in a year, give each partner church the ability to "double its income, size and miracle ministry." In that order! We're growing; in income and size and power, but at what price? At the cost of the broken and wounded we trample and neglect on our way to successful Christianity? God NEVER intended this. HUMILITY is the mark of grace. "Not I, but Christ." "I must decrease, He must increase." Look at what we're doing: are we really walking in that understanding? God is going to have to take it all down, all the flesh and pride projects, and make them fail. As it comes down, God will raise up a humble grace-filled people to whom Jesus is not a way to succeed or be blessed or any other thing, but He is their all-consuming passion and love for whom they would gladly give their all and seek no return! To serve Him is reward enough. "For then I will take away from your midst those who rejoice in your pride, and you shall no longer be haughty in My holy mountain. I will leave in your midst a meek and humble people and they shall trust in the Name of the Lord. (Zeph. l:3:11-12) We must be broken to receive grace. This should be our cry: "If You aren't going with us, DON'T LET US MOVE A STEP FROM THIS PLACE. If You don't go with us, who will ever know that we have found grace in Your sight, and that we are different from any other people on the face of the earth?" (Ex. 33:15-16) How, indeed?

A DIFFERENT FACET OF GRACE

The receiving of grace is an effortless act that comes from becoming desperate enough to come to the cross for it. But the WORK of grace - that is, the ongoing transformation - is not easy at all. Grace challenges us to our full potential in Christ. Salvation grace releases us from the penalty of sin - abundant grace equips us to become "more than conquerors." The moment you ask for the ABUNDANCE of grace, the Holy Spirit begins radical renovation of your life and circumstances, because you have in effect asked Him to make you like Jesus no matter what it takes. Grace will change you - not coddle you - it will shatter the old man and drive you to your absolute limits. Old reliable talents are shelved - new ones are given. No wonder we'd rather stay in the shallow craters of grace! To receive abundance of grace is to know that "You are bought with a price, you are NOT YOUR OWN." Grace is the determined power of God to enable us to live extraordinary lives. That grace is no soft thing, but puts us in the midst of humanly impossible situations and empowers us to endure and be victorious, giving us courage, making us resilient, unstoppable, immovable, indestructible saints!

Our understanding of grace has to go beyond asking for strength when our blow dryers go out or we have to wait in line at the bank. Dark days are ahead for the world and we've got to go deeper. "If you have run with the footmen, and they have wearied you, then how can you contend with horses? And if in the land of peace, in which you trusted, they wearied you, then how will you do in the flooding of the Jordan?" (Jer. 12:5)

THE SCHOOL OF GRACE

The school of grace is a very private and individual. It's a little like the educational program that lets you work at your own pace. Sometimes we have to retake classes until we get it right. There's grace for failure but not for those who do not even try. Grace allows you to learn from failure.

"How come things seem so hard to endure, and when I ask for grace it doesn't get easier?" Which of us hasn't asked that question? Recently, quite by accident, I was visiting a friend and watched Karate Kid 1. There was one scene in it that riveted me. The young boy had asked the old man to teach him Karate; he agreed, as long as the boy did what he said without question. He then handed the boy rags and set him to washing and polishing cars. When he finished, exhausted , the old man gave him a paint brush and told him to paint the fence. He did, came back, and he was told to paint the other side. He finished and angrily told the old man he was just using him. The old man told him to show him how he waxed the cars, the specific method - then how he painted with a deliberate up-down stroke. Then the old man began shouting those instructions fast and hard, at the same time attacking the boy with karate blows - each one met and blocked perfectly by the boy's moves! All of a sudden, I understood - the tedious and endless tasks, the discipline of the Word of God when there was no strength...it was grace at work! Grace disciplining me, stretching me to my absolute limit, causing unseen growth, preparing me by grueling challenges for purposes not yet understood! Grace is the power to endure! It is the Spirit's cry from your guts when everything inside is trembling that screams, "FINISH THE COURSE!"

I'm not given to dreams, but recently I dreamed about the two precious ladies who were my deaf choir directors, who had taught me the hard facts, in words and their example, about the challenge of true ministry. In this dream, we were on a high and dangerous roof. One of them began to fall. I went into action, and with several intricate moves, sat her safely down on the roof. She stood up, pointed at me and said, "No! Don't you understand? I didn't want you to make me safe - I wanted you to make me STAND!" It was a lesson from God I so much needed! You see, there is so much lack of love in the world that we surely have needed to bring people into the security of God's love, and ours as a church. But we cannot stop there! As wrong as it is to tell people what to do but not loving them enough to walk them through things, it is even more dangerous to establish them in love but overprotect them, shield them from reality, not causing them to STAND. To GROW UP! This is NOT a safe world, and it's going to get a lot worse before He returns. God's primary purpose isn't making us feel safe - it is to cause us to stand. Stand up! Hothouse Christians cannot stand on their own, choosing and preferring to just "not deal" with the reality of this desperate world we live in. But GRACE is the POWER TO STAND. Grace does not pad your reality. It places you in the big middle of the mess and says, "Stand up!" and then gives you the power to do so.

THE OUTWORKING OF GRACE

As you dare ask for abundant grace beyond just grace for salvation, many changes will come. Grace will "Strengthen and build you up" (Acts 20:32). Grace is an increasing work. "Grace for grace" or "grace exchanged for greater grace." (John 1:16) The more grace received, the greater the challenges, and the greater grace to meet and be a conqueror with each challenge.

Abundant grace is only received where needed and sought for. We must become needy to receive it. "The people who survived the sword found grace IN THE WILDERNESS." (Jer. 31:2) In the dry desolation of human failure and the end of flesh striving, we cry out and receive grace and rest.

Grace is not a one-time event. We must "Continue in the grace of God." (Acts 13:43) It is a day by day dependence, where we are not one bit stronger without Him today than the day we first believed. We are not one ounce more worthy of His love. Departure from daily grace will become a return to the law, legalism, striving and pride.

THE OUTPOURING OF GRACE

Grace in Greek means, "Graciousness, especially the Divine influence upon the heart, and its reflection in the life." If grace is real in us, it is reflected and manifested through us to others. The outpouring of grace becomes the outworking of grace (sanctification) which becomes the outgiving of grace to others. You can tell the degree of grace a man has received by how he treats others. Legalists, gossips, the intolerant and proud, judgmental and self-righteous have never gone beyond the shallows. Grace is evident by the amount of giving, forgiving and love poured out. The nature of God's grace is "undeserved favor". When I look at our selfish, possessive, clannish, cliquish church and family examples, I grieve to see we have only cared to receive grace for ourselves - we are grace-hoarders. Grace MUST give out. Don't ask for abundant grace unless you're willing to lay down your life for the brethren.

Gregory R Reid

THE FINAL CHALLENGE

I want to end by challenging you. There are only two kinds of believers: those that press on in grace and courage, and those who draw back in selfishness and fear; those that dare to give their all, go the distance, and those who cling to their squatter's rights and won't move; those that cling to security at the price of stagnancy, and those who take the challenge of the 100% life of holiness and love regardless of the price. Hear the Word of the Lord: The children of Israel were about to possess their inherited land and cross the Jordan. But the tribe of Gad would not go! They pled with Moses: "If we've found grace in your sight, do not take us over the Jordan!" (Nu. 32:5) Jordan is the death of the self-life each believer must face if he would move on. To them grace was an excuse to avoid going on, dying to the old nature, an excuse to cling to their worldly safety no matter what! Moses said, "Shall your brethren go to war while you sit here?" Their selfish cry was a discouragement to those going on. Today we see it so often: A husband or wife desiring to go on with God but the spouse doesn't want to give up "the good life". A church, cautious and authoritarian, stifling those who would dare to do something radical for the cause of their Savior. Moses' message was basically, "Stay then, but don't get in the way of those who want to go on." They lost; they settled for a worldly inheritance.

I challenge you to examine your own heart: Is grace your excuse to avoid 100% commitment? Is it your escape from reality? Do you value security above giving your all, taking up the cross and laying down your life for the brethren? Do you ask for grace to avoid the fight, or the grace to be strengthened to fight? "As your faith is, so be it unto you." God will give you as much grace as you dare to receive, or as little as you long for. But if we as the church would ever hope to be more than a self-centered, self-important, powerless organization, we must dare to receive the "abundant grace" to become the life-changing, light-bearing, Christ-centered" people we were meant to be.

9 THE LAST DEFILE

We need to talk about death. We do not think about it when we speak of healing. It haunts us, stalks us, puts a weight on every life decision. But for the believer, death should not be dreaded, as if it were an end, but welcomed, because we are going Home.

But why don't we feel that way about death? More Christians than not dread the thought. Few know anything about what heaven will really be like. Most just stay busy to avoid giving it much thought at all.

Beyond surface reasons Christians fear death, I believe there is another motive behind our sweeping the inevitability of death under the rug: it is not the fear of where we are going as it is of what we may leave behind: a wasted life! What did I accomplish? What is precious, what is chaff? What could I have done, what could I have been, if only Christ had really been my commander-in-chief? "The world has yet to see what God can do in, and through, and with a life that is completely and totally consecrated to Him." (D.L.Moody) Did I even come close to grasping what that means? How will my friends and family remember me? Will it be with deep grief but joy, grief at the separation but joy that there were no regrets, no unfinished business, only precious memories and the knowledge that I finished my course well? Or will it be bitter tears at the things I left undone, the love I failed to express, the words I did not say?

I'm beginning to think mid-life crisis is merely the halfway point where all life's priorities, failures and dreams are suddenly shoved in our face. Childhood cemented the material, which would, for good or bad, make us adolescents; and the choices, right or wrong, which we carried out in the crucible of adolescence paved the road for the careers, relationships and decisions which carried us to this mid-life point. Youth has faded. Some cheat on their loved ones trying to recapture the thrill of young love; but it fails. What is past, is past; we begin to fear the future because there is LESS of it than before, and the greater the sense of personal waste, the more gripping becomes that fear of tomorrow - and death.

At whatever age that revelation comes, you reach a crossroads: to turn back attempting to recapture past success and vitality, or to plan the years left in order to be fruitful, eternal, valuable and enduring. No matter what your age, it is not so late that those years can't be tremendously important and fulfilling. Remember - Abraham wasn't exactly a spring chicken when God gave him his greatest work! But pity those who waste more years trying to relive their adolescence, or those who blindly think a career change will quench the burning fears inside. Only an offering of those remaining years to the destiny of God will bring true peace.

They say man's greatest needs are to love and be loved, and to have a purpose. Focusing on the third, life for most of us is 90% busy work and 10 % true purpose, if that much. We're so busy "getting there" we forget why we're going! Thus the tremendous emptiness of recognizing life is coming to a close; thus the dread fear of dying without leaving a spiritual legacy. Life, work, school, careers and entertainment are total vanity without the knowledge that we are to fulfill a God-given destiny. Solomon wrote a whole book on it, Ecclesiastes. He, who had wisdom, pleasure and riches, said he'd done it all and it was worthless! One wonders, with all due respect, if he hadn't forgotten his own destiny as righteous heir to David's throne. There's a key here: for many the fear of death can be directly linked to the fear of leaving no decent spiritual legacy.

Many years ago, I shared intimately in the death of the woman who raised me in the Lord. She was a simple woman, never married, who was a bookkeeper. She died with more pain than I'd ever seen anyone endure - and she died fearlessly. She died knowing she had finished her course and that a glorious place was waiting for her. Her fearless passing helped me overcome my own fear of death.

While sorting through her things, I found two things that helped me understand how she could be so fearless. First, was a note she had written to herself when she knew she was dying. It read: "Chemotherapy? At most one year either way. Don't want to burden others." Even in her darkest hour, her thoughts seemed to only be not wanting to be anything less than a servant. Incredible! Then, I found a stack of letters her "boys" sent her year after year - a group of young kids she had taught the Bible to when she herself was barely a teen - nearly seventy years later, they still wrote to tell her how much her caring had meant! I can't help feeling part of her fearlessness was because she knew she was leaving a rich legacy in Christ in those she touched. I know, for I am one. This, from a woman whose outward life appeared so menial! Again, there is no one too old, too beset or too discouraged to fulfill their destiny! I only fear death if I feel I've left no spiritual inheritance to those I love. Solomon found his life worthless because he'd wasted it all on self-indulgence. He'd so thoroughly forgotten his destiny that he allowed his godless wives to erect baby-sacrificing altars to demon gods!

Another key: Solomon was a self-serving man. Naturally he faced death empty, because we only carry out of life what we have given away to the Kingdom of God. I wonder if many of us ever go beyond our securities and creature comforts to understand the truth written, "Only one life, will soon be past; only what's done for Christ will last." To know that destiny and fulfill it is to be able to face death with assurance of His care.

None of us know how long we have until the "last defile". My grandmother outlived her own son; a friend died at 16. It's unwise to not at least acknowledge our mortality. A good dose of truth about this inevitable event (the death rate IS still one per person) can actually help us refocus our living and reorder our priorities. Put another way: If you had one year left, how would you spend it? Give that some sober thought. I would ask God to make it the most fruitful year of my life. I'd get my affairs in order and out of the way. I'd write long letters to loved ones, telling them what they mean to me. I'd tell those who know Jesus to love and serve Him with all their hearts. To unsaved loved ones, I would preach the sermon of my life about salvation. I'd visit everyone I could. I would write with every spare moment, knowing words often speak more powerfully after we're gone.

I would tell my friends to grieve, because it's silly not to. It devalues the preciousness of the relationship not to grieve. "Be happy - he's in a better place!" I may be, but we sometimes cry even when a loved one moves or goes on a long vacation - why do we deny the living tears for the loss, even if it is temporary? Plus, I find it hard to believe I will not miss those I leave, too!

That all sounds noble and romantic. Maybe I won't be so brave or selfless if I find I do have one year left. But it's good to live as if today IS my last day. It tends to change my priorities. With the knowledge of life's brevity clearly defined, I can make determined decisions, as if today were all I had. I'll start each day with Jesus, asking Him to use me and love through me. I'll keep in mind that each word I speak in haste, anger or bitterness could be the final memory another has of me. Therefore if I do speak unkind words, I'll resolve them immediately. I'll remember no work or project is more important than time spent with those I love (unless God so requires). Work is endless and temporal: only Jesus' love shared is eternal. I will never forget that "all that matters is that which is eternal." I know living life with such clear priorities isn't easy, but it's the only sane way to live. When it comes to relationships, we always think, "I'll resolve the conflict tomorrow." "I'll apologize later." "I'll write them next week and tell them I love them." Knowing you have no guarantee you'll have the chance is a sharp reminder to do it today.

Aside from all the above, I find many Christians who live godly, fulfilled lives still fear death because they don't understand it. It's not taught, at least not well, in churches. Our usual concept of eternity is ethereally floating, bumping into stars, or sitting around singing Amazing Grace for millions of years. (Having a voice somewhat like Bob Dylan crossbred with an alley cat with asthma, this prospect doesn't excite me much.) Let me share some things that have truly given me joy about what is to come.

1. We will have a body "like unto His glorious body." In Jesus' resurrected body, He ate, drank, walked and touched. "Touch me and see I'm not a spirit". Paul said we desire, not to be unclothed, but to be further clothed. Our bodies define us in a way, contain and identify us. Rather than being body-less, we'll have perfect bodies - no pain, no shame, no humiliation from age or deformity.

We'll eat foods never before imagined. We'll see smells, taste colors, touch music. We'll know each other - not less than who we were on earth, but more - in perfection - without the human anguishes and sin to keep us from each other, and Him.

2. I think many fear that heaven will be less than earth, because "spiritual" really means "less" to us. The woman who raised me in the Lord used to look out over her mountain home and say, "If the earth is this beautiful under a curse, imagine what it will be like when the curse is removed!" What an insight! Earth, with all its marred beauty and pleasures, brief glimmers of love, belonging, joy and nobility, is merely a shadow of what is to come! No tears but those of joy, no loneliness or sorrow, where children run free and Jesus walks by our side! All that man longs for - love, belonging, acceptance, peace - all this heaven is, and more. How can we believe that God who has given us so much on earth could ever make a heaven that was in any way less? I cannot fear knowing that!

The same woman who taught me not to fear death left me an incredible story. A man was dying. The doctor came to his home. Even though the dying man was a Christian, he was terrified of death. He asked the doctor, also a Christian, what awaited him at death. The doctor hesitated, trying so hard to find the right words to release this man from his fears. Suddenly, there was a scratch and woof at the door. It seems the doctor's dog, who has been left in the car, got out and found his master. The doctor opened the door, and the dog leapt on him and plastered him with a wet tongue. Then the doctor knew he had the answer. "Joe," he said, "My dog had never been in this house. He had no idea what was on the other side of the door; he only knew his master was there. We don't know exactly what death is all about - but you can rest in knowing that Jesus is waiting on the other side!" This precious reality should quench our fears. Jesus - our Savior - our Beloved - waits for our coming with joy. He'll be there, and the longing of every man's heart will finally be fulfilled - we will be Home! That longing, that aching loneliness and pain of feeling lost and alone - gone forever, swallowed up in the arms of Jesus.

Do not fear death. Live to fulfill your destiny every moment and finish your course with joy. He is here now, and will be there to carry you to a home so unspeakably beautiful that all life's pain will be gone in an instant. "Death, where is your sting? Grave, where is your victory?" Thanks be to God for His unspeakable gift!

Make us Thy mountaineers; we would not linger on
the lower slope,
Fill us afresh with hope, O God of Hope:
That undefeated, we may climb the hill, as seeing Him
who is invisible.

LET US DIE CLIMBING.

When this little while Lies far behind us, and the last
defile Is all alight, and in that light we see Our Leader
and our Lord, what will it be?

- Amy Carmichael -

10 BITTERSWEET

I just read a quote from someone that has me thinking. The quote had to do with the difference between "salt" churches and "honey" ones. I don't know what point he was trying to make, but this is what I heard: Salt churches are ones that speak truth harshly - "without compromise". Honey churches always sweet-coat truth so people will swallow it - or worse, just feed them honey and skip the truth altogether.

Thinking about this disturbed me because I'm under constant self-examination about how I handle people. I used to be a Bible-basher. If it was in the Bible, I would defend it, preach and "proclaim" it. Which is good. But my heart grew proud in the process. I'll never forget giving a 3 hour seminar in California. My teaching was stout, clear and unbending. After, the pastor told someone, "He's so holy, it scares me." Maybe you'd be complimented but I was terrified. I knew pride came before a fall. Plus, I knew my own heart. I wasn't as holy as I sounded, especially since the filth of pride and self-righteousness permeated my heart.

I softened up since then. Sometimes I've wondered if I've gotten too soft. For a while, I was listening to some pretty "humanistic" voices. I still defended God's Word, just less loudly. In an effort to understand people's hurts, I got too quiet about truth. I guess that's a typical Christian pendulum swing. I became a honey Christian. I was afraid to tell people the truth, even in love, because they had been hurt by Bible-bashers. I put honey on kernels of truth. Sometimes I skipped the kernels altogether.

I used to be very hard on one young man who later backslid. I softened up in the meantime. We talked for a few months frequently, and he began to tell me about a sin he was engaged in that he had honey coated somehow into being not-sin. I swallowed, took a deep breath and told him the truth - gently, in love – that he was sinning. He was floored! "I thought you'd changed. Now it's obvious you haven't." I told him, "My approach changed, but I haven't changed my stand on God's Word one bit."

We don't talk much anymore.

I felt later I had been a little dishonest. I hid behind being a "good listener" in order to avoid telling the truth. Why? I wanted to be liked. And, I was so sensitive to hurting people that I was more concerned with their feelings than with God's.

I'm still midstream in God's dealing with me on this, but here's what I've learned so far:

1. TRUTH HURTS. As long as there is sin in us, it will hurt to be faced with it. As someone said, "The truth will set you free, but first it will make you mad." Or miserable. Or both. But we've got to face facts: man's nature is to avoid facing himself, or God, or truth. "Adam, where are you?" "Hiding." "Why?" "I'm naked." God knew that. We run, hide, justify; why? John said it: Because of fear. Fear carries with it the expectation of punishment. Oh, we're so much like the little boy in the tree saying, "You can't see me, my eyes are closed and it's too dark to see anything!"

You know what I'm afraid of? I'm afraid we've gone to bending over backwards to make people feel O.K., so much that we've buried their wounds, not healed them. Man is NOT O.K. He's sick, sin-bent and self-destructive. But that doesn't mean he's not loved! You see, when we tell people they are O.K., loved "just the way they are" then the next step is for people to think, "I'm wonderful! I deserve God's love – I deserve His best!" How frightening. People begin to expect from God what all saved sinners should only gratefully - and undeservedly - receive.

I've come back to the truth that only when man understands the depth of his depravity, sins and utter helplessness without Jesus can he ever know the tremendous life-giving gift of undeserved favor and love given at the cross.

The Prodigal Son didn't come back saying, "Well, I was struggling with self-image, I had to 'find myself'. Yeah, I made some boo-boos but I discovered the good in me and so I'm back. Sorry if you got hurt." It went instead like this: "Father, I have sinned (personal responsibility and facing the truth) against heaven and in your sight (he recognized sin is NEVER what you do to yourself - someone else is always hurt - no man lives, or dies, as an independent person) and I'm no longer worthy to be your son. (He threw himself at mercy's feet with no bargaining chips.) Make me as one of your hired servants. (The pain of sin had humbled him so much that he was willing to accept ANYTHING but rejection!)

The father didn't say, "It's O.K. son, you just needed to find your potential, get some possibility thinking going. You were O.K.. all along. You didn't really sin, you're not really unworthy." No. It was understood by both: the son DID sin. He WAS unworthy. The glory of it, a glory so many of us try to rob people of, is that despite ALL his sins and unworthiness, he was forgiven completely, no questions asked. He could come home. In fact, because in the slime pits of sin he faced his sins ("he came to himself"), because he faced it and didn't hide, he was FULLY RESTORED.

We preachers don't realize the crime we perpetrate by not helping people face themselves. We rob them of the precious experience of full pardon. Instead of producing Davids by saying, "Thou art the man," we produce Sauls who run around saying, "Doesn't anyone feel sorry for me?" I'll be honest - the life-changing moments in my life were when God showed me my own heart, either alone in the prayer closet or through another when I was too blind to see. (I prefer the prayer closet!) TRUTH HURT ME! But oh, the release that came! The relief! Because truth is just the sword that cuts deeply enough to allow healing oil to be poured in.

2. Telling the truth is not yelling and making people feel guilty.

I've been quite devastated by some very soft-spoken words. "A soft answer breaks the bone." A loud, haranguing preacher isn't automatically a "prophet of righteousness," neither is the Anointing to be judged by the decibel of the preaching. Such a preacher may be getting a secret thrill out of yelling at people - you know, sin is what *you* do that he *doesn't*. We've got to be full of love when we tell the truth. "Mercy and truth are met together; righteousness and peace have kissed each other." (Psalms) The two, together. Never forget, we're to be the salt - not the vinegar - of the earth. Moody said, "If we must peach on hell, we might at least do it with tears in our eyes."

3. You don't have to honey-coat truth. Someone said you can catch more flies with honey than vinegar. I have to wonder what anyone would want with a church full of flies anyway. We should always be sensitive to people's needs, but not so much that we slight God. Always honeycoating truth or just pouring on honey to make people feel good about themselves, we're "healing slightly the hurt of His people." You don't give aspirin alone to a cancer patient. You don't give a little Band-Aid to the blind and bleeding.

4. There IS honey to be had. But it's found IN THE ROCK. Inside the unbendable truth of God's Word is the sweetness of grace.

I guess some hard-liners will be thrilled by what I just said. Not so fast! Truth alone does not heal. The letter can KILL. Some of people kill with truth. They prefer calling people perverts than making them converts. How wrong they are. Jesus said, you do all the right things but neglect mercy and

61

justice. The truth needs to search, convict and break your heart before you EVER point your finger at the next person.

I hesitate to use the word balance, because I tend to agree that it usually is a code- word for compromise. But I believe there IS a balance between salt and honey. In Exodus, Moses brought Israel from the Red Sea and they were in the wilderness 3 days without water. They came to Marah but couldn't drink the waters because they were bitter. (Marah means bitter.) Moses cried to the Lord and God showed him a tree, and when the tree was thrown into the water, it became sweet. (Exodus 15:22-25)

Sin has made the water of life bitter. Moses didn't say, "Oh, we'll just find sweeter water." They had to face the bitter. They either found a way to drink it, or died. We have to face the bitter fact of sin's destruction in our lives first. But there is a tree...it is called Calvary. That tree shows us truth and the reality of sin's horrible consequences. But when we throw that tree into the bitter waters of our lives...when we come to that place of Calvary and receive His forgiveness, the waters become sweet!

We need to stop lying to people about the bitter waters of sin. Stop leading them to "sweeter" waters. Several decades ago, a false prophet named Jim Jones killed almost 1,000 people with sweet, sweet Kool-Aid - laced with poison. Many of man's ways are sweet-tasting but poisoned waters. But when we face the bitter waters, really facing our lostness and sin, there is a tree, where Jesus King tasted and drank the full cup of sin's bitter water. The cross is the only healing, the balm, the honey. It's only for those who come naked, "Just as I am, without one plea." If you try to circumvent the cross you bypass the only cure and your honey will become a bowl of vipers.

I want to be a "bittersweet" believer - a salt *and* honey Christian. Sometimes someone does need just honey. I don't want to pour on salt when they do. But I don't want to baste someone in sweet words when they need the sting of truth. I'm committed to finding that "balance" without compromising God's heart. I'll have to become less fearful of being disliked, more willing to be cut myself, more sensitive to what is needed most in any situation, listening for that "word in due season" whether it interferes with my planned speech or not. I'll have to be more into God's words than man's ideas, to "cease from man whose breath is in his nostrils" and stay close to God whose breath is in *me*. Truth in love - it is one word - separated, they become two counterfeits - truth which is pride and fear in disguise - or love which is compromise. The salt and honey - truth and grace - the judgment and the pardon - the water and the tree - to be whole, holy and loved, you must know both. If you know just one, you'll be a proud lawgiver or weak and immoral. God give us grace to know both.

11 THE BLOOD OF ABEL

How long, O Lord? How long? Lord, the children are crying. The youth are dying. How long will You hear their cries, and not answer, not act? They are being slaughtered on altars real and humanistic, and we turn away. HOW LONG?

I once prayed great, elaborate prayers, impressive and strong. Now my prayers have become shorter...trembling. I have seen things no man can endure without being changed, and I understand Solomon's words: "He that increases knowledge, increases sorrow." (Ecc. 1:18)

It began for me in 1987 when I met the parents of a little boy who had been molested and forced to watch Satanic sacrifices at the hand of an "innocent" daycare teacher. The parents were overwhelmed with anger, disbelief and pain. But I was not prepared to look into the face of a innocent little boy's eyes and live with the haunting anguish of knowing what he has suffered. How long, O Lord?

Then I stood at the graves of Shane and Sally. Still young teenagers, they got into the wrong crowd and were mutilated, tortured and shot to death. Scores of kids came to their graves that day to cry, to find some reason WHY, and to them was given two brief and vague messages about the afterlife by two preachers who barely knew them and even mispronounced their names on this, their last day of remembrance. How long, O Lord?

Over the years, I have traveled and seen things no one should have to see. I have seen young people with empty, dark eyes and mutilated hearts who never even heard that God really, really loves them, and will take them just as they are. I have seen little children who have been abandoned, sexually abused, satanically used and ruined for life, unless someone brings Jesus into their terror and pain.

My call to God's work began when I was just 16. In a year, two things would mark me with God's heart-print for life. First, there was Jimmy. He went to our youth group. At 13, he was so closed off and shattered that no one could reach him. Later I learned the youth leader's husband, a pillar of the church and boy scout master, had molested Johnny. I said, "God, I want to be his friend." And we did become friends. He was my first "son in the Lord." Last year, I saw someone in the airport that looked just like

Jimmy. My heart leapt and tears came to my eyes. It wasn't him. But I realized that, many many years after I had last seen him, I still loved him and carried him in my heart. I always will.

The second incident that changed my life as a teen happened one day on the way to work. I had just picked up my mail and was sorting through it on the way. Someone had sent me information on the horrors of kiddie porn. Enclosed were just the faces of some of the kids they were using. I pulled over and cried so hard I hurt. "God," I cried, "Take my whole life! Use me! Help me to help these children, to stop their pain!" It was a costly prayer but I do not regret it for a moment. Everything I do has the unchangeable mark of these two encounters.

I could not have known then how much worse things would be in this hour. God partially prepared me once in a dream. In it, David Wilkerson (Teen Challenge founder, a man God has greatly used to mold my life) said, "Son, I have to show you something." He took me into a viewing room, turned on a movie projector and showed me a porn film of adults and BABIES! I cried in horror, and David went into a rage of grief, smashing the projector and ripping up the film. Since that dream in 1974, I knew the day would come when man would become so evil as to do this to children. Today they make these very films. How long, O Lord?

For many years, my heart has been poured out and agonized over the children and the youth. I have wept as case after case of child brutalization has been thrown out of court and the abusers set free. I have listened to, cried with and held so many young people who have had lives so tormented that I could barely sleep for thinking about them. I have held an eight year old so terrified of evil that he could only cry in utter fear, a fear so deep that it wrenched my spirit until I nearly vomited. How long, O Lord?

I was part of the great Jesus movement. It was pure and God-breathed. And I watched it die, as controllers and hucksters choked it to death. In 1984 I had all but given up hope, until God gave me a prophetic dream of young worshippers, hand in hand, in the midnight hour raising tear-stained faces of love to the Father. Then one young person, crying, said, "Please pray for me. It's so hard on the Jericho road!" I awoke, my awakeness less real than my dream, and I begged God once more, "Use me! Let me see it once more. Help me reach the hurting kids!" I know God is not through with this generation!

I will never forget the night an 11 year old was kidnapped by a masked stranger. This went right to my deepest heart. All my knowledge of

Satanic cults led me to believe the worst for him. I became almost obsessed with the case, the boy's face on my mind, his picture on my wall, his name constantly on my lips in prayer. Every time I passed his picture, I wept with a pain that felt like I'd been kicked in the gut. I can't even describe the helpless pain I felt, knowing that a merciful end for this child would be preferable to the torture he would be enduring if he were still alive. How do you pray for that? Am I making you uncomfortable? Then let me tell you of an encounter I had over Christmas. At my hotel, I saw a young boy of about 9 and his little sister waiting by the gift shop. I looked into their eyes and saw a well of fear and pain so deep that it literally took my breath from me. Something was horribly, horribly wrong! Then I overheard him tell her, "Face it, Sarah, they've left us. They're not coming back for us. We can't even go home now." By the time I had gotten security, they were gone. How long, O Lord?

I've faced many enemies over the years. There are people who want me dead. There are "experts" trying to smear me to promote themselves. I don't really care. It's part of the cost. Only one thing troubles my spirit and breaks my heart: A Christian world that chooses to turn away!

Oh friends, wake up! Don't you see what is happening? The Satan who has always killed children because they are innocent and destroyed the youth because they are the future is now devouring them both like so much grass because we are not standing in the gap for them! So many times as I've shared the ugly realities of the destruction of our youth and children, people have just glibly said, "You're just glorifying the devil." Or worse, "I'd rather not hear this." How long can we turn away, refuse to see and turn deaf ears and refuse their cries? The blood of Abel cries again from the ground of our bloody nation. Rachel is once again weeping for her children, for they are no more! And we, who have the only answer, continue to insulate ourselves with creature comforts, petty selfish personal problems and phony religious entertainment! Fiddling while Rome burns, we continue to dance even though the music has become a funeral dirge!

The youth are searching and desperate, but our only concern is doctrinal rightness, making sure we look right, talk right and don't associate with "sinners". HOW LONG, O LORD?

One last time, God says, He will call, He will move. Gone are the days of power entrusted to the spiritually selfish. Those who choose to stay selfish, myopic and cloistered, be it believer, leader or church, will be left to dance their delusion alone until the end. But even now, God is saying, "Who will go for Us? I'm preparing a feast. Call whoever will come. I care not how ugly or sinful, crippled or wounded. I love them! I will heal them! Compel them to come!"

The multitudes of wounded wait. Who holds the answers for abused children? The courts? No! Hear God's Word: "He pronounces judgment on the judges. How long will you judges refuse to listen to the evidence? How long will you shower special favors on the wicked? You are so foolish and ignorant! Because of you, all the foundations of society are shaken to the core." (Psalm 82:2, 5 LB) There is no hope in the courts! There is no hope for today's youth in self-help programs, psychology or secular education! They are empty! They are lost! What is the answer? Is there hope? Yes! But only if YOU respond to the battle call. Why is the church the last place kids go for help? Could it be because they have had so much rejection already that they dare not face it from us, knowing that if God whom we represent rejects them then there really is no hope? 95% of the kids I've met who are involved in the occult were raised in church! But they only saw those who "have a form of godliness but deny the power thereof." The only hope they have is in real Christians willing to pay the price to love these kids into healing. Will you? Or, will you stand with those to whom God speaks this awful indictment: "The people of Ephraim, though fully armed, turned their backs and fled when the day of battle came." (Ps. 78:9 LB)

The battle is here. You are fully armed even now! You have the Creator in you! You are the only hope for a lost generation! Will you go, will you pray that most dangerous prayer, "Whatever it takes, Lord, use me?" Are you willing, as Amy Carmichael said, to let your house be a little more empty that His house may be fuller? Are you? Or will you plug your ears to the cries of a lost world while Satan eats them alive?

Last week while teaching on the God who gives justice to the orphan, fatherless and oppressed, something came to me, and I leave it with you.

It is Solomon's observation, more clear and true each day: There is no justice in the earth. But even though this is so, God wants you to know beyond any doubt: There may not be human justice for the abused, the hurting, the abandoned and wounded. But there can be love. And healing. IF you let God love and heal through YOU.

Will you?

12 PUT THE AWL TO MY EAR

"Search my heart, O God; try me, and know my anxieties; and see if there is in me any wicked way, and lead me in the way everlasting." (Ps. 139:23-24) I run from that soul-searching.

Over the years Jesus has been pulling me aside from the big ministry I once knew, dismantling my inbred ideas of ministry. He taught me bigness isn't greatness; that busy-ness isn't necessarily faithfulness; that church has to be more than a place we meet, and that passion for God and fervent love for each other is His highest desire for us.

I'm in a new classroom; the lesson is servanthood. In a time when shepherds have become kings of privilege to be sheltered, exalted and followed, I've had few examples of real servants to learn from - but what an incredible few! They have been windows to God's heart for me, whose lives taught me what serving is.

My first lesson was being called to serve another ministry where I learned there is only ONE ministry - Jesus'. It's hard to compete when you learn that truth. I think Paul understood that when he replied to accusations from Christians, "At least Christ is preached!" I long to come into that kind of understanding, and having been in and even formed competitive ministries, I long to be free to abandon myself to HIS place for me, no matter how small it may be.

When the Lord asked me to call off a ministry trip to stay with a sick friend, it was a personal breaking. It was a bad career move for one whose year's schedule had only this one trip to count on for maintaining visibility! Most American ministers, if honest, would admit like me that obscurity is fearful and feel they must keep their hat in the ring somehow! The week at the hospital was powerful. I knew Jesus wanted me there, and I knew it was more important to Jesus than MY plans. One night outside the hospital the questions weighed heavy. "Why am I on this earth? Why did You take me from public recognition to almost total obscurity?" As Jesus searched my motives I hated what I found. My planned trip was based on fear of being forgotten, and its purpose (no matter how spiritually disguised - I must be honest with you!) was at least partly to raise money for a financially hurting work. Even deeper...I wanted to go someplace I could be appreciated, honored, used greatly! To SERVE in OBSCURITY was not something Bible School ever taught me.

The questions continued: What is it to really serve Jesus? The church seems to be caught up in everything but Jesus. Money, rivalry, pride...competition...causes...new theology. It was complicated and confusing. Where were the real servants? Wasn't anyone just talking about Jesus anymore? As I kept watching the rise and fall of Christian evangelists, the more I heard Christian leaders come up with answers: "We need more accountability." "We need holiness!" "We need to pray more!" Some truth to them all, yet I felt we missed the real need of the hour, as we tried to put a Band-Aid on a deeper problem, a problem executive decisions and surface cleanups will not heal. What is needed is people of genuine Christ-like character, and believe me, that has got to go far beyond looking good on the outside - it means genuine love, compassion, selflessness and truthfulness. We've fed our new ones so much about miracles, gifts and such that we've failed to tell them God's heart is that we be like Jesus, and all else will come from that. Of all Paul's prayers, the one that seems to speak so poignantly to the need of the hour is, "I agonize like a mother in labor until Christ be fully formed in you!" Does it really matter if we do His miracles and teach His words, but people do not see HIM in us? Locally a group from a "prosperity" church came to a restaurant and left behind an angry group of waitresses who heard all the talk of Jesus but only remembered the rude treatment and a tip so minuscule it was an outrage. Charles Swindoll tells of a beggar to who went to ask for food at an inn called "St George and the Dragon". The rude proprietor called him names and told him to leave. The beggar returned a moment later, and to the owner's shock said, "Well, if St George is in, can I talk to him instead?" Our character MUST match the words we say! I'm not speaking of perfectionism or false holiness, but of lives that are compassionate, kind, patient, truthful and vulnerable, brave, noble, giving and without pride. It is a lofty ideal, but isn't it time we realized Christ has called us to represent Him in the way we act, how we live and treat each other? What do we look like to the world? Do we look like Jesus at all?

During the hospital time, one of the nurses observed the care and loving interaction of friends and family for our bedridden brother. He was drawn to us, and we hope will be to Jesus, because unbeknownst to us he was seeing what Jesus said would be the real mark of Jesus in us: "Behold how they love one another!" What matters is the caring, loving and serving others see that will really draw the lost!

I have looked in the wrong place for examples. For I now know the real Jesus-like servants have been there all along - rarely in the high-profile arenas, but in hidden corners! Unspoken servants! Unlauded giants. They serve in rest homes and by building houses for poor people. They bake bread for sick neighbors and hug lonely teenagers. They are silent heroes, obscure warriors who only serve and don't even regard their own service. These time-tested servants will stand tall when the megachurch is dismantled and forgotten. These saints have been sprinkled in my life all along, from a dear old saint who raised me in Jesus to a pastor who taught me grace by walking with me in a time of failure, to a friend who took me in when I was homeless. They all looked a lot like Jesus to me! As I look back on many years of sermons, messages and conventions, I remember few if any words. All I remember is the Jesus-like people who hurt when I hurt, gave from their poverty, faced me with gentle truth and said with their lives what Jesus' love is like. The only sermons I remember were those precious moments when they showed me Jesus with their caring love. I long to be like that; I often fear my epitaph will say, "Here lies a great teacher" when it should say, "He loved others like Jesus did."

The obvious next step is that rather than decrying the lack of examples, God is saying, "You be the example!" This is where maturity lies: to release others from our expectations and blame and cry out for freedom from the wounds we take when leaders fail, and determine we will be that servant of love! Yes, we will first see how bankrupt we are in ability to love, but God counts what we have and not what we don't, and with just a willing heart, it becomes the explosively powerful touchstone of God's grace to be what we are called to be.

Out of this came an understanding of how little the world notices a difference in us. We're just like them in the way we relate, raise money and treat others. We've worked hard to create programs and music the world can "relate" to. Which requires a constant update of current trends and fashion. Watching Christian music videos the other night, I was amazed at our accuracy in imitating the world and its shallowness. "Alternative entertainment" for kids? I suppose it does have a value not unlike miniature golf or a trip to the water slide. But ministry? Hardly. And you know, I really don't think the kids respect our attempt to "relate" to them. Go to a local kids' hangout - same clothes, sunglasses, language. They face a severe identity crisis: Who am I? How do I look? Do people like me? Here I come with the same clothes, hairstyle and talk. Do you think they are going to look to ME for an example when I'm just like them? They need a role model, not someone that is so insecure I look as identity lost as they are!

Let's translate that to the larger picture. In the guise of "trying to relate to people" we've become simply a trend-conscious imitator whose real motives I fear have less to do with making the Gospel relevant than it does simply revealing our own wounded identity, longing to be accepted, important, respected. We don't know who we are! A person secure in their identity in Jesus doesn't need to imitate, look like the world or "make truth relevant" for truth is eternal and love cuts through any facade, as well as exposes the absence of it.

My friend and pastor Rick Howard often quotes from a child's book, *The Velveteen Rabbit.* I thought it a bit strange to see this tremendous teacher so moved by such a story, but perhaps only now when I'm older can I understand, for some understandings only come with age. The story is about a new stuffed rabbit, discarded in a closet, where he talks to an old worn out stuffed horse that had all but fallen apart. "What is 'real'?" the rabbit asked. The horse replied, "Real isn't how you're made...it happens to you. When a child loves you for a long, long time, not just to play with but really loves you, you become real. Generally by the time you're real, most of your hair has been loved off, your eyes drop out and you get very shabby. But those things don't matter because once you're real, you can't be ugly except to those who don't understand."

Maybe this was a word just for me but its message undid me because I see our desperate need to be real - not slick or professional, full of facades and masks we put on T.V. Not imitators but original, unique Jesus people! Not trendy, always theologically correct, not mega preachers or Dove award winners- just simple, real servants who no longer regard how people see them but only want to love like Jesus.

I told this story to a young man I taught and prayed for earnestly the last two years. I spoke of my pastor friend who had been like a father to me. He interrupted me, looked right into my heart and said, "You've been like a brother to me." It was hard to contain my tears, for as anyone who touches young lives knows, these are moments that make caring worth any price. God, help us to know how you count on our hands, arms and hearts to touch people! I saw in that moment with my young friend the passing of a precious torch - a real man of God had been a father to me and taught me to be a real Christian - and now, I saw that love had made me a real brother to my young friend! One day, he will love another and thus the real Kingdom grows. My friend may not remember many of the words I've said, but he will remember who I was with him, what I was to him. Suddenly the multitude of words, debates, Christian wars and trendiness mean nothing to me. For I have been loved by Jesus through others and others wait for the torch to pass from my own heart.

Perhaps this all seems like the ravings of a bewildered saint. It doesn't really matter to me if this word has been a little disorganized because words can't contain the cry of my heart for you to understand the part you must play, His cry for real Christians, true servants. Each of you can make an eternal difference for one life! As the mega monolith falls, Jesus is calling His "little people" to fill this long neglected place of personal caring that no television work can truly do. Yes, you'll make mistakes and fail people - but somehow if someone knows you love them, those failures don't seem to matter much. Amy Carmichael's biographer said she once thought Amy could do no wrong, which was good at the time, but later loved her more seeing her mistakes, because she saw it was possible to follow such an example who was so human! Our acts of love overshadow our imperfections. Another story is told about a soldier in post war London who saw a small boy, almost starved, looking hungrily into the window of a bakery. The soldier asked if he would like some pastries, and he eagerly replied yes. The soldier bought them, gave them to him. The boy looked up and said, "Mister, are you God?" Oh, that we would grasp how much people need to see Jesus caring though us!

An Old Testament slave, when he was free, if he chose to remain a slave because he loved his master, had his ear put to a wall and pierced with an awl and given an earring to signify that he was a "bondslave" - a servant of love. In an age when real servanthood has yet to be modeled by many leaders, when cleansing the outside of the cup has left neglected the matter of true integrity and Christlikeness, when being trendy is more important than being real, when young lives cry for real identity and only see imitators of their own confusion, when love is rarely taught as the most important virtue and seldom walked out for others to see; O Lord! Put the awl to my ear. Teach me to abandon myself and find my identity in You alone. May I become real - because of the years of love so tenderly poured into my life by those whose humble service, though never lauded and seen by few, have shown me Your heart. Let me pass that torch, one at a time. May my life not be marked by eloquence nor success as men count success, nor any other thing but the earring of love that shows I am Your servant and thus the property of all, not one to be served but to serve, not one to seek to be loved but to love - not to seek my own glory but only to honor You - not to seek to be known but only to live so others may know you.

Gregory R Reid

13 COVENANTED TO WAR

I learn a lot from worship services. Every service has its own feel - its own emphasis - its own weapons. They can simmer, smolder like a quiet fire, rage with the flames of heaven or fall cold like the icy breath of hell itself. Someone recently told me he can walk into a worship service and tell where each person is at. I've found that to be true. Some are so bound that worship just annoys them, there are showoffs who have one eye closed and one opened to see who's watching them worship - or see who isn't worshipping. I've concluded it's a mistake to think praise and worship are the same thing. In our minds, if there's a difference, it is that praise is fast and worship is slow. But I believe both are war tools, but the real profound difference is that praise frees us, but worship frees God in us! Praise cleans out junk, lightens our burdens. But worship brings His power to bear upon us. It frees God to empower us to war. When the angels hear true worship, they come to attention and stand ready to battle for us and alongside us. Knowing that worship and praise is not only an intimate communion with God but also a war cry, we need to then ask, "What is this war about? What are we fighting for? How do we war?" The answers may surprise you.

First we are at war for a lost world. Satan owns this world system without contest - unless we contest it! I'm a great believer in taking territory from him. However, not like some who put up billboards saying "Jesus is Lord over____" (Put any city's name) and simply want to build big buildings, prosper their businesses and be influential socially while the homeless still starve and the drugs flow and the kids die on the streets. No, this war is much more personal than all that, this taking of territory. God isn't into taking over physical cities nor Satan interested in having just the physical places. (He's got plenty of desert to hang out in.) It's the people Satan is craving like a meal, and people that the Lord Jesus longs to come and dine with! If the territory we seek to repossess is the human heart, we are with God's heart. If we just want to feel important and prove we aren't social nerds, we're out of God's will in a big way.

We are to reclaim the territory of human hearts, then. Until we understand that Satan's only way of hurting God is to hurt those He loves and died to save, we will never understand the real heart of evangelism. It's not about numbers! It is a caring, compelling compassionate commission from the heart of God for the one!

Let's take it a step further. For years I've watched new babies birthed into the Kingdom and die. We're so interested in numbers that we tend to just leave the new babes to fend for themselves. Spiritual crib death results, leaving hundreds of thousands of people with one-time born again experiences who never grow to maturity, even when they're "plugged in" to a church, because most churches are missing the one ingredient essential to strong life - discipleship. That's a scary word that just means someone has taken responsibility to raise someone in the Lord. Face it - most churches aren't designed that way. The pastor does - is expected to do - it all. Most church people are too busy and self-absorbed to even think about caring for someone outside their nuclear family. But the church won't go on without it! "Hey, we got 100 new souls!" But how many lived? Grew? Went on to fulfill their destiny, raise up others? Isn't it a bit like, "The operation was a success, but the patient died"?

Back to the war. Something very real has been given into my heart by the Holy Spirit recently. It's about covenant. A covenant is a commitment, an agreement, a contract, a promise. The whole Bible is about covenant - old covenant - a new and better covenant through the blood of Jesus. Covenants were sealed in blood. We just barely understand the power and awesomeness of our blood covenant with Jesus. Let me explain what I understand about human covenant according to the Old Testament times, and perhaps we can see what God is after. When two men, leaders, people or tribes "cut covenant" with each other, they brought the people together, sacrificed an animal, walked around it, cut wrists, and made a vow: (Hear this carefully) "All I have is yours. If someone hurts you, they hurt me. If someone hurts your family they've hurt mine. If they war against you, they've made war with me." Besides marriage, it was the most serious earthly covenant made. David and Jonathan were covenant brothers. Ruth an Naomi were in covenant: "Where you go, I go, your people shall be my people and your God my God. God forbid that anything should part you and I." These were intense covenants, made and sealed in love. The kind of covenant God wants us to have with each other!

In a way we should all be in covenant with believers. But there is a deeper more personal covenant, one you can't make with a billion Christians. But you can covenant with a few, or one, can't you? But our problem is that we covenant with no one outside our flesh family. It's easy escape to pay a preacher to do it. But if we are to become a mighty army, we can't do that anymore. I hear a lot of people crying for kids to be raised up as warriors. Here's the problem: You can be a soldier and not love your fellow soldier. But you can't be real family without loving each other. We're trying to raise kid warriors but they end up off & alone & blown to bits because God's army is only effective if they are first family, if they are looking out to protect and defend the brother or sister in arms next to them! Satan doesn't fear soldiers - he fears family warriors!

Why is this so important to this last hour? Because this is the most wounded generation in history, heart-wounded, taking pain killers and covering up their devastation. We're trying to take kids right out of the hospital onto the battlefield while they're still bleeding! No! We have to get them healed and strong first. Also, this generation can't be reached by more seminars, hyper activity and war cries, they need honest role models - vulnerable, caring, committed –warriors of the heart! No hype, no "trying to relate," just real caring people willing to commit for the long haul.

I guess you understood when you read how covenant took place that it is made relevant to us by Paul's words, "Rejoice with those who rejoice and weep with those who weep." And again, "Who is weak and I am not weak, who is offended and I do not burn with anger?" Now we've come to the heart of the matter. How can we battle for the lives of unbelievers if we don't war for each other? Years ago I was watching the news and God spoke to me so clearly! Kuwait was just invaded by Iraq. The commentator said, "Even though there is an agreement between Arab states to defend one another, all the Arab states are reluctant to interfere for fear of their own invasion." That's the church! We *say* we're in covenant, but we don't lift a finger to battle the devil for our brother when he is being besieged!

God is looking for warriors. Especially youth warriors. But I don't know one man or woman God greatly used who did not have someone in their lives who cut covenant with them, who said with their words and their lives, "I'm here for you. I'll pray always for you. All I have spiritually is yours. You matter to me! We belong to each other, and I will defend you with my life." Distance and time doesn't change the covenant, for it is eternal and timeless.

I have been blest by such saints. I would have become a worthless wounded soldier left to die, but God chose for me a white-haired saint who saw my need and my potential and covenanted in her heart to be my mother in the Lord. She called me when I was away from God, opened her home, her heart and her treasure of wisdom and God's love to me, and because of that, I am a warrior. When it mattered to no one but God if I made it, it mattered to her! I still have a handful of real covenant family who battle for me and I for them. I couldn't do what I am doing without their war pact.

I believe God is calling every mature believer to covenant with another. God will not allow His war to proceed with uncommitted soldiers, or with soldiers without anyone covenanted with them! How do we start? By asking God to give you just one life, one young believer you can commit to. It's not mechanical, it's a thing of the heart. If you dare to ask God to show you one person, God will bring them and birth such a fierce love for them that you will know this is the one to whom you are sent. Yes, it's costly, it will hurt, it causes sleepless nights and agonizing intercession. But the covenant God requires is a covenant to war - to war for one life "Until Christ be fully formed in them". Dare to be a heart-warrior, dare to care for one person and see them raised up a mighty heart-warrior in this end time. This is what Satan fears the most, for when we begin to tie together the cords of this covenant, with one, then another, then many together, he knows we will not, cannot be stopped. The battle will be ours!

14 JUST A BIRD

It was just an accident.

A tiny little Cockatiel who hopped around - well, walked, really - and sat on your shoulder and pulled on your earring or hair and wolf-whistled during Bible study and carried on trying to join in during worship at the home of her loving owner. The little bird was greatly loved by her owner. That night, the little bird was kept in the bedroom for safety, since she had no cage. The kids were told not to go in there. One disobeyed, and crushed the little winged creature to death under an accidental -yet disobedient - misstep. He was mortified. He was twelve.

The owner, who had seen a lifetime of tragedy, loss and death, cried bitterly and openly, inconsolable. For you see, the bird was a joy in an otherwise painful and dark world. It was a little ray of God to her. A thing of innocence.

The kids' reactions were mixed. Most stood by helpless, not knowing what to do. The shock for me was hearing of one saying, "What's the big deal? It's only a stupid bird."

In those words, I heard the voice of an entire generation. In that evening's events, I heard God speaking about disobedience. And in that bird, I heard God speaking about innocence and loss.

First, disobedience. This is a generation without rules, other than convenience and "what's right for me". It is a generation reaping the destruction from that horrible breach of God's laws.

We so wrongly look at God's Law and say, "It's just too hard. God loves me, right? But the law seems so cold. So restrictive. So impractical." But why is it there? For our protection. The law is fixed. Like gravity, it just is. "The soul that sins...it shall die." Why? Because sin destroys. God didn't say "don't" because he enjoys seeing us restricted. He said it because sin kills. My generation, which largely discarded the law of God in favor of pleasure and self, only partly reaped the results. It is this generation where the full holocaust of disobedience and sin is clearly bearing fruit. Ask why God gave us the law, and then look at the consequences of raising kids to disregard that law: AIDS. Drug abuse. Kids who murder their parents.

Kids who don't care.

Kids who can't feel compassion, or pain, choosing rather to numb themselves with drugs and sex and violence.

We didn't mean to raise this generation to turn out that way. Neither did the young boy mean to kill the bird. He just wanted what he wanted, to do what he wanted even when he was told not to. But you see, we're so bound to ourselves, so narrow that our first thought is always about "me." What will God do to me? How will I suffer? But it wasn't the boy's bird that was killed. Someone else paid for his disobedience.

This generation is paying a high price for our disobedience! Sin is never just about me. Everyone pays, as David found out in the whirlwind of violence his adultery and murder produced for generations to follow. "You have sown the wind, and will reap the whirlwind." (Hosea 8:7)

Next, there's the comment I heard. "It's just a stupid bird." A generation who cannot feel for the least of God's creation will likely feel little for people, either. "It's just a fetus." "He's just a nigger." "They're just a retard." Do you see? We're seeing now the full fruition of disobedience in our nation: Social numbness. We are becoming a people so pleasure-mad that we're little different than wealthy Romans who attended the arena slaughter of undesirables and Christians as a social sport. Actually we still have them. They're called "talk shows." When I see cross-dressing strippers, a 16 year old who has had 30 women in his bed, and partners who videotape sex applauded wildly like heroes, I know we're way beyond the point of no return now. The intolerable is now accepted. Blatant law-breaking is accepted, excused. How can children raised by Tabloid TV *not* be numbed and without any sense of truth and reality?

I'll never forget the dream I once had of people who were bloody, dismembered and nearly dead. I said, "What's the worst thing about the Antichrist?" "He doesn't let you feel," one answered. TV remotes are like a morphine drip! Watch one minute of suffering on the news, turn the channel, there's comedy central. Don't feel.

In my work with abuse victims, numbness - not feeling their losses - is the worst kind of suffering there is. Pain proves we're alive. In my work to stop satanic criminal groups, I have seen numbness to the full measure. To them, children are animals to be caged and killed - and, like the bird, something innocent to be crushed under their unfeeling feet.

One of my greatest agonies about working for children and families of abuse in the system is how the numbness is there, too, in the system. Children are for many just case files. Lose a case, return the child to the abuser. Oh, well. Next case on the docket? "It's just a stupid bird." "You can't get personally involved." One of my greatest griefs is knowing the extent of abuse and slaughter of innocents and knowing so much of the church is turned to Holy Ghost Partying rather than feeling God's pain and doing something!

No, it wasn't just a bird to me. It was a symbol of innocence. President Clinton spoke after the Oklahoma City bombing about our loss of national innocence. It's been lost for years, Mr. President, we just can't feel anything but major shocks anymore, and then just briefly. Click. Back to Comedy Central and the Playboy channel. We've got to wake up!

Last week, I was gardening, when a bird hit my sliding glass window. I ran over, praying it wasn't dead. Now, this may sound strange to those who know I'm a devoted blackbird killer. Well, they're predators. They kill and eat smaller, helpless birds. But this was just a defenseless little creature. I picked it up. I was sure it was dead. I prayed for healing. I wept. An eye opened. After a while, praying all the time, he managed to perch one foot on my finger and I held it steady. There it stayed for a while as I talked to him, prayed for him and he slowly regained consciousness. He did not fear. Then I put him on the ground, and he hopped, then flew to a little apricot tree in the corner of my yard, then after lingering a while, flew away.

I wept because it was a deeply tender moment in a brutally callous world. I wept because he was so helpless - so dependent on my kindness, so vulnerable to my possible brutality. And I wept because I heard Jesus say, "How can you think, if you feel so deeply for that little bird, that I don't love and care for you a thousand times more?" Does He really care that much? Yes! And if He does, what kind of agony does he feel for the battered and defenseless of the world? And knowing He does, how can I ever turn away from the call to bring healing to all I can in His Name?

Gregory R Reid

15 PADDED ALTARS

I sat in the pew, waiting for the altar call. Suddenly my eyes were fixated on the altar before me - a padded altar. Nicely carpeted, to prevent knee pain. It was to me a picture of our soft faith. It hurt to see it.

It hurt because it exposed my own love of comfort, hatred of inconvenience. It hurt because we are a nation of padded altar Christians. We protect our knees from pain as we pray to the One with thorns deeply gashed into His brow, whose flesh was torn savagely off His back, who was spat upon and hung to die.

I think of Amy Carmichael of Dohnavur, India, who left home and comfort for a dangerous, demon filled land to rescue children destined for temple prostitution at age five. She faced constant criticism from religious people and losses human and physical, yet she only asked to be used. She counted the cost and disregarded it. Us, well, we want to know, what's in it for me? Chances of success? Salary? Benefits? Inconveniences? As long as the benefits - personal, that is - outweigh the inconveniences and costs - count us in to serve the Lord!

I'm not trying to be judgmental. These things judge me, too. But I'm troubled, and I'm wondering, why are we so ineffective at reaching a lost generation?

DABBLERS?

I work with kids who are suicidal, Satanists, drug users, from broken homes, scared, scarred, angry, lonely and lost. The world rejects them for trying to be Christians, and many Christians reject them far the way they look, act, or because they're still falling, still in pain that makes them lash out like wounded animals. Sure, I'd like them to be well now, but if it takes years, so be it. It's worth the cost.

In the meantime, it is so troubling to go to city after city teaching on the dangers of Satanism and hear officials, religious folk and educators say, "All we have is kids dabbling." And my first thought is, well, a dabbler today can be a murderer tomorrow, so deadly is the occult drug. And my second thought is, why do people treat this like it's barely worth our attention, just because it's kids? Aren't they our future? Shouldn't you be doing SOMETHING to help these kids get out??? Then I remember the padded altar, and the revelation came: If there weren't so many Christians "dabbling," there would be a lot less kids "dabbling"!

What is a Christian dabbler? It's someone who only considers God when it's convenient. It's someone who says, "God, I'll call you when I'm in trouble," and runs their own life the rest of the time. It's a fad-oriented Christian who looks for things to amuse, things to keep from boredom, who get hooked up with "new and exciting ministries," support them with undying loyalty and finances until the thrill wears off and the thought of actually having to work and get one's hands dirty and have their time tied up hits them, at which time they drop the ministry like a hot rock. Christian dabblers are best described in Madison Avenue terms: "Try Jesus." Well, He's not to be tried. WE'RE being tried! And we are being weighed in the balance, and we are found so lacking in all that is true and eternal. Jesus isn't a quick fix for our ills. He hasn't redeemed us to fix us. (That is a natural result of His love.) He has redeemed us to love us, for us to love Him, and then to out and rescue others. Christian dabblers try a little Bible, a little church, but never enough to change how they live and love. The Savior of their soul soon becomes "The man upstairs" - vague, distant and powerless over their hearts and affections. Dabblers dispense money, time and Christian caring like a hoarded treasure. The idea of 100% ownership by Jesus Christ hasn't occurred to them.

By contrast, kids who dabble in Satanism, fpr example, only increase their commitment to it, the same as kids dabbling in drugs, alcohol, etc. While they are dying from "dabbling" and being dismissed as not that important, Christian dabblers just STAY dabblers, their commitment to Jesus does NOT increase. No wonder the kids don't listen to us. As one girl said, "How do you expect me to believe your God has power if YOU don't believe it?" These kids are committed. But us, well, Jesus is just part of our lives. He is not our life. And the only hope the kids have is seeing a stronger commitment to Jesus than they have to self-destruction.

2 KINDS OF SATANISTS

If you can't relate to why people follow Satanism, prepare for a shock. Christian dabblers have within their breasts the same motivation of a Satanist. For the law of the Satanist is, "Do what thou wilt." Satan's falling sin was pride, selfishness, wanting to do what he wanted, not what God did. And before you shake your head in disgust at people who worship the devil, just remember that when you do what pleases you only, when you run your own life and give passing lip service to God's will, when your selfishness hurts others, then you too are "doing what thou wilt" and act with the same sinful heart that a Satanist does.. The only difference? The kids are usually honest enough to admit who they serve, while Christian dabblers are deceived into thinking they're good religious folk. Do you see why the kids disregard our message?

Well, maybe that's too much for you. But you need to wake up to see the battle for this generation is real. Do kids see anything in us that might give them a shred of hope that their lives can be different? Are we different enough from the world and its rejection and fear and false securities and sick values to say with our lives, "We live like we believe"? Are we?

I recently spoke with some dear church ladies who shamefully admitted that long-haired, ear-ringed kids wouldn't be welcomed in their church, fearing they might have a bad influence on their teenagers. And I said, "Then it has failed to be what God wants. It says that your kids are so weak in faith that they need protecting. They should be so strong and on fire that the worldly kids should need protecting from THEM or else JESUS will invade their turf!!"

In a padded altar age of Christian Trivial Pursuit ("Do you have to speak in tongues to be Spirit-filled? Do you believe in once saved always saved?") I leave you with a challenge. It's best illustrated by our altar calls. It recently occurred to me that perhaps we're raising halfhearted youth and halfhearted parents and halfhearted believers who are half committed because we have misrepresented Jesus at this very altar. Every head bowed, every eye closed, no one looking around...and then, those words are spoken that must sting Jesus' heart: "WE DON'T WANT TO EMBARRASS ANYONE, but if you want Jesus, just slip up your hand and put it down quickly...." What, so no one has to see you? What are we saying to people in this eternal moment? That Jesus is not worth being embarrassed for? That you can make a neat, no-embarrassing decision that no one has to see? Oh friends, look at it! Look at Jesus! Our Beloved, stripped naked, dripping with blood and spit, speaking forgiveness. Is this not the most embarrassing shameful moment of all? Don't you think this is worth not just a quick hand, but worth running to the altar for? Worth any and all embarrassment? Don't you see, we ourselves are telling people by this padded altar call that a hidden commitment, a half-hearted prayer is OK? It's NOT OK! You can't reach a generation of kids committed to self-destruction without a commitment that doubles their own, a commitment in love to Jesus who gave it all, all! Stop dabbling with Jesus. Strip the padding off the altar of your heart! Let your light shine. Let them know Jesus is worth it all!

Gregory R Reid

16 SOCIAL SERVANTS OR BONDSLAVES?

Being in ministry isn't what it used to be! Years ago, priorities were clearer, black and white were more easily seen. The Gospel was a thing both hated and respected. People had real needs and the answers were there in the Word of God if you looked, knocked, asked.

Today, everything is upside down, backwards, inside out and lost in space. For any thinking, truly seeking Christian, America is clearly a bizarre mix of Disneyland, hell and the Twilight Zone. To survive is to fight hard and brutally. To survive and be truly effective warriors, God has to strip you of all the illusions, delusions and teach you to walk with your heart and head in another Kingdom.

Today, you must fight to keep your priorities clear. Into the gray of compromise, God calls you to paint life with strong colors - not just black and white, the colors of truth, but also sunset reds, forest greens, brilliant yellows and sky blues, the colors of grace. God calls you to break the spell of evil and delusion and walk out of Disneyland, taking captives with you. In a world where the Gospel is no longer hated and respected but rather amusing and mocked, (God-bashing is in) God calls us to an integrity, a nobility, a royalty that exposes darkness and by its nature demands a strong reaction for or against our God and Savior Jesus Christ.

Today there is a mass deficit of true servants of Jesus. Those I know who have crossed Jordan, who have prayed to be used cost what it may, are overloaded. Why? Supply and demand. The demand for true servants and true service is far greater than the supply, so the overflow goes to the few who serve. (Forgive my long explanations. After taking 5 minutes to explain this theory to a friend, he condensed it to, "So God has a management problem." I wish I were so brief and clear. But then, I have both sides of this page to fill.)

Then, those who ARE servants are faced with challenges of time, energy and anointing that are unbelievable, because for so long people's needs have been unmet by secular psychology, social Christianity and the Band-Aid counseling of this generation of "care bear" Christians. When servants are called along these hurting people they realize that they cannot heal with just a nice bunch of words or a few easy scriptures. "Social servants" quote a verse or two, pat people on the back and say, "Be warmed and filled" feeling good that they have done their good deed for the day. Bond Slaves are willing to commit to the person for Jesus' sake, they dig in for the long haul, they make the person's healing as important as if it were their own. They cry for them, they weep for them. They are willing to lose a little sleep if it means bringing the other person into His rest. They are willing to let their house be a little more empty that His might be fuller. They are willing to give you their heart, no matter how you hurt them, so you may receive the love of the Great Heart of God.

I was recently telling some friends about the tremendous increase in responsibility and work we're facing. Someone joked about being fired, and I said, "You can't fire me. Slaves have to be killed off or die to quit."

Suddenly the joke becomes a dead-serious revelation. Suddenly I saw so clearly the difference between a hireling and a shepherd, between a career oriented professional preacher and a true Jesus-servant, between a social servant and a Bond Slave of Jesus.

We're always faced with the contradiction, the huge gap between where we are and where we need to be. The truth is that hidden, selfish motives are something even the most committed Bond Slaves must keep in check. After all, being raised in Disneyland means we've been raised an media trash like, "You deserve the best" and "I'm worth it" (Some have even built churches on these premises.) But if we're gutsy enough to face the lies, God will deliver us and make us the true servants He needs. Our greatest enemy is selfishness. It comes in two forms: doing nothing unless it's convenient, or the way many churches have developed, letting the pastor and a few elders do it all while you pay them 10% to do so. "Pastor Cork." We put him at the top and we remain bottled up until out of frustration we blow the cork out (usually into another job) and the people just lose their fizz! Funny, how Monday morning commentators set up the heroes then shoot them down for failing to meet their expectations.

In God's true order, pastors and leaders are not elevated heroes but just servants. And the purpose of service is to mature other servants. The problem is, most of us don't *want* to be servants. We want to pay the Pastor to serve! Part of the reason leaders are stressed out, burned out, fed up and sometimes even quit is because they are doing the work that should be done by *all* the people. It's time for God's people to stop playing "poor, weak little lamb, help me!", stop expecting others to wait on you and please you, grow up and start serving! Technically, according to Acts, leaders should be giving themselves to the Word and prayer. That's their primary job. For the church to grow, for the Good News to spread, you must relinquish your padded pew privileges and do it! If you're willing, here's a few guidelines to help you exit Disneyland and enter the real battle, helping you to see the difference between social servants and Bond Slaves.

1. Social servants say, What's in this for me?" Bond slaves say, "What can I give?"

2. Social servants say, "I'll do it if it's convenient." Bond Slaves say, "I'll go when God calls, convenient or not."

3. Social servants say, "Why should I do it? No one else volunteered!" Bond servants say, "No one else volunteered, that's why I'll do it."

4. When the going gets tough, social servants get going - far, far away, and fast.

5. Social servants become "cruisematics" - when a church "stops meeting their needs" they move on to get fat and lazy elsewhere. A Bond Servant, when their needs stop being met, realize they have what they need and they start meeting others' needs, right where they are.

6. A social servant excuses self, blames others for failures and lack of involvement. A Bond Servant says, "Search *me*, O God" and "Create in *me* a clean heart."

7. A social servant is blind to their own faults, but considers themselves an excellent judge of the faults of others. A Bond Servant realizes they are responsible that they themselves walk uprightly, and should they see a fault in others, they recognize that it has been shown by God so they may pray for them or lovingly correct them if necessary.

8. A Social servant does the minimum required to get by while making every effort to receive the maximum credit for the job done. A Bond Servant excels in all things, especially serving, and if possible without getting attention or praise for it, for they do it to love Jesus.

9. You have to drag, bribe or draft a social servant into battle. You have to kill a Bond Servant to get the sword out of their hand.

10. Social servants are "excitement addicts" who attach themselves to new and exciting works of God, pledging their loyalty, until things get boring or costly, and they move on quite quickly, searching for the next "fix". The Bond Servant feels they *must* serve. They are grateful to be

chosen to serve. Excitement or not, they serve steadily and consistently. Social servants plant a tree and get mad if there's no fruit in a week. Bond Servants know good fruit takes time, lots of water and sunshine, and even if no fruit is seen soon, it may just mean the roots are going deeper down.

As time passes, the fruit of the heart becomes known. A social servant becomes increasingly meaner, prouder, more petty, selfish, critical and eventually bitter, lonely, empty and barren. But a Bond Servant becomes the Living Tree of the fruit of the Spirit: kind, selfless, constructive, sweet, full of love and greatly blessed.

You can remain a social servant. You'll get to heaven empty-handed. You can expect, claim and demand blessings. But at the end, you'll know what Jesus meant by, "They have their reward already." Even here, you will understand the stark pain of Psalm 108:15: "God granted their requests but sent leanness into their souls." And you will never understand the true blessings only Bond Servants know: To enjoy God's friendship; to know God is trusting you; to have God share with you His secrets, His heart, His longings and burdens; to be so confident of God's favor that you dare to speak the truth in love without fear of being disliked or rejected (social servants are trained in flattery); to be blessed with lifelong relationships with other Bond Servants that time, distance and circumstance does not dim; to have your capacity to love be ever expanded, deepened, enriched, and finally, to know God's "thank you" far letting Him love through you!

You may not measure up. Few do. We're not there yet, but like Paul, we don't consider ourselves to have arrived, but we press toward the high calling. But you're willing! As you grow in grace and understanding of these things, you will see changes that assure you that you're getting there. You start thinking of others' needs more than your own. You actually go out of your way to comfort and be a friend. You begin to feel others' pain. Your prayers are less you-centered, more for others, and just praying to bless God and love Him. You even start losing sleep praying for others. Instead of trying to get others to meet your needs, you're beginning to lead others to, and back to Jesus. You no longer need to be asked or bribed to help, you do it with joy. You're no longer asking to be a better Christian (which is often disguised selfishness - you know, if I'm more holy, I'll get my prayer answered and people will think highly of me) - but rather asking to be a better servant, by which being a better Christian is produced. Your priorities become His - heal the sick - take care of the oppressed and orphaned and widowed -seek justice and extend mercy.

May God give you the grace to understand and obey. Goodbye,

Disneyland. Welcome to the real world!

Gregory R Reid

17 WARRIOR'S CREED

1. JESUS IS NOT PART OF MY LIFE!

Jesus IS my life. I will not give Him 10% of my money, time or obedience. By His grace, I will lay my life down at His feet and give Him 100%. I am not my own.

2. I WILL WATCH MY WORDS.

Proverbs says that life and death is in the power of the tongue. More people have been destroyed by lying, criticism, judgmentalism and gossip than by many wars. Before I speak, I will weigh my words, and the consequences. I will pray, "Set a watch at my lips, O Lord."

3. I WILL VALUE SILENCE.

The more a person talks, the more it shows how empty their heart is and how shallow their relationship with God. I learn far more from listening than from talking. I will listen to others - there are far too few listeners. And with my Father, I will listen as much as I pray. He wants to talk. I cannot expect guidance or comfort, challenge or growth if I simply hand God my wish list and walk away. The world is too full of noise. I will remember that when God spoke to Elijah, first there was a whirlwind, then a fire, then an earthquake, but "The Lord was not in them." Then came a still, small voice. I cannot be greatly used unless I take time to listen.

4. I WILL VALUE ALONENESS.

This is the loneliest generation in history. We are so afraid of being alone that we will take any friendship, date any person and go any place just to make sure we aren't alone. But I accept that loneliness is a gift. It is God on the telephone. Even if I have friends., even if I marry, there is still a God-shaped loneliness which will never be completely filled until I am with Him, but which drives me to His heart while I am in exile here. I will set apart time without T.V., without radio or music, without people and without hurrying, to just be with Him, worshipping Him and loving Him. A great leader once said he would not see the face of man in the morning until he saw the face of God. By God's grace, this will be my goal as well.

5. ALL THAT MATTERS IS THAT WHICH IS ETERNAL.

I will set my affections on things above (the things Jesus cares about - success, money, power, etc.) I am determined not to be counted among those who have just enough of the world to be miserable with Jesus, and just enough of Jesus to be miserable with the world. I will count myself as a pilgrim and a stranger in this world and strip myself of every worldly entanglement I can, so I can please Him who has called me to be a soldier.

I will not sacrifice eternal reward on the altar of temporary pleasure. Knowing that the great tragedy of judgment day will be what I could have been if I had let Jesus really run my life, I will keep a daily awareness that only those things I do for Jesus will never be forgotten. Because I am away from my real Home, wherever I find a true believer and share in the fellowship of God's love, they will be my home.

6. I WILL LET LIFE BREAK ME, NOT HARDEN ME.

Jesus said the rain falls on the just and the unjust. I expect hard times, and I am determined to let no circumstance make me bitter, or hardened to God, or unwilling to love. In any trial, I will ask Jesus to let it make me into a broken servant. Only when I am broken, am I strong.

7. I WILL HAVE AN HONEST RELATIONSHIP WITH GOD.

Jesus said I must worship God in spirit AND in truth. I will hold nothing back from God. I will yell, scream, cry, laugh, tell the ugliest sin and the deepest hurt to God without reservation or fear, knowing He already knows what is in my heart. I will eliminate all "thees and thous" and formal nonsense from my prayers and simply talk to my Father as I would to my friend. He is not frightened or offended by my anger or my honesty, nor ashamed of my tears and my wounds. I will hide NOTHING from Him, and even when I have sinned, I will take it to Him right now.

8. I WILL ASK TO SEE AS JESUS SEES, AND HEAR AS HE HEARS.

Knowing that "man sees the outward appearance but God sees the heart", this will be my goal as well. I will judge no one by their dress, words or actions, but will ask Jesus to show me their heart. A prophet is one who "sees with seeing." God, help me to see as You do, hear as, You do and feel as You do, as well as think as You do.

9. I WILL NEVER DENY IN DARKNESS WHAT I KNOW TO BE TRUE IN THE LIGHT.

The truth of God's love, Jesus' power and my purpose are easy to stand for when things go well. By God's grace, I will never deny these truths no matter how much my personal fires and trials may seem to say God does not love me, that Jesus cannot help me or that I have no purpose. "Let God be true and every man be a liar. Though my faith in these truths be tested, I will spit in the devil's face and tell him, "Though He slay me, I will still serve Him."

10. I WILL NEVER ASK WHY - I WILL ONLY ASK WHAT FOR.

I am not exempt from suffering or problems. Therefore, when they come,

I will not ask God, "Why me?" but ask Him what the trial is meant to produce in me. "Why?" is a pointless question. But "What for?" allows the Holy Spirit to use the circumstance for my growth and guidance.

10. I WILL ACCEPT ROMANS 8:28 AND NOT CURSE MY PAST.

If I really believe that "God is at work in all things to produce good" then I accept that there are no exceptions. Therefore my past, no matter how painful, ugly or sinful, can be transformed into a tool of compassion and forgiveness that the Father can use to touch hurting people.

11. IN THE HEALING OF MY WOUNDS, I WILL NEVER GIVE UP.

I accept that hurts that took years to form may not change overnight. There will be spiritual surgeries and times of tears. I will not settle for a halfway deliverance, but seek God's face until my emotions are fully healed and in God's hands. A former prisoner war once asked how he endured all the years of imprisonment and still had hope. He replied, "I never decorated my cell." I will not become comfortable with my wounds or the sympathy my flesh seeks from them, and I will not decorate my personal cell of pain, I will be free.

12. I WILL PLACE OBEDIENCE ABOVE ALL HUMAN OPINIONS

AND EXPECTATIONS.

Although I will listen to all criticism, receive and weigh all counsel, I will not allow anyone's opinion to deflect me from following Jesus and His will for me. I will always play for the Coach and never for the crowds. Knowing that popularity is not approval from God, I will not allow man's praise to feed my ego nor his blame to defeat my spirit. Only Jesus' opinion counts.

13. I WOULD RATHER MY NAME BE KNOWN IN THE CORRIDORS OF HELL - AND FEARED -THAN BE THE MOST POPULAR, LOVED PERSON ON EARTH.

Knowing that God's Kingdom and message is advanced more by prayer and obedience than by personality and persuasion, I am committed to making sure demons know I mean business, not to impressing the crowds.

14. I CHOOSE TO BE ALONE RATHER THAN PARTICIPATE IN CHEAP, SHALLOW, EMPTY, FLESH-BASED SOCIAL FELLOWSHIP MANY CALL "FELLOWSHIP".

Paul said, "From now on we know no one after the flesh, but after the Spirit." I will not waste my time socializing but find and addict myself to Christians whose life is lived in the love of Jesus and His calling.

15. I WILL SEEK TO BE VULNERABLE AND TRANSPARENT COST WHAT IT MAY.

If Jesus lives in me, then I do not want people to have to sort through the trash in my heart to see Him, I will seek to be cleansed from all secret sins, so that I am like a clear window through which my Savior can be seen. I will not be afraid to share my heart, my healing or my struggles, if that will gain the trust of the wounded, so that I can take their hand and place it in the Father's healing hand.

16. D.L. MOODY SAID, "THE WORLD HAS YET TO SEE WHAT GOD CAN DO IN AND THROUGH THE PERSON THAT IS COMPLETELY AND TOTALLY CONSECRATED TO HIM, AND BY GOD'S GRACE, I WILL BE THAT MAN."

By God's grace, I too will be that man. I want no other thing than for God to use my life as completely and thoroughly as He can, and whatever price I must pay to be that pure vessel, I will pay it and not shrink back.

17. I WILL BE A "SAFE PLACE" FOR HURTING PEOPLE.

The world is full of betrayal of trust and of innocence destroyed. I realize, in the words of Floyd McClung, that people don't care how much I know until they know how much I care. Therefore, I will seek to be a trustworthy friend and a person who will not condemn or turn back from anyone's sins or problems, but rather give them a place where they can know the completeness of God's acceptance and love.

18. I WILL VALUE THE ONE OVER THE MANY.

Knowing that Jesus left the 99 to seek the one, knowing that Jesus always took time for the one person who needed Him, I will not prefer crowds to the one life Jesus may give me to love and disciple.

19. I WILL NOT KEEP MY DISTANCE FROM PEOPLE WHO ARE HURTING.

I will be willing to get my hands dirty and get into the blood and mud of their lives to bring them to Jesus' arms. I will not be afraid to cry, for tears are precious to God, and only an insecure and proud man cannot and will not cry. Paul commanded that we weep with those that weep, and I will ask God to break my heart until my tears become powerful intercession on behalf of the hurting soul. Knowing that only a man afraid of himself will not show gentleness, I seek to know God so deeply that I can say, like David, "Your gentleness has made me great." Knowing that God longs to bring people to him "with cords of human love." (Hosea) I ask God to let me be the cords through which His love is shown.

20. I WILL PASS ON THESE TRUTHS.

Jesus said to make disciples - followers of Him. Knowing that Jesus has given me, through spiritual parents, a great legacy, I will seek to instill that legacy into all those He gives me to raise up. Then, I will teach them how to pass it on to those they are called to. I will never forget that God's Kingdom is a family and only grows as I am willing to lay down my life to raise those He has given me to love for His sake.

21. THE GREATEST THING IS LOVE.

Knowing that 1 Corinthians 13 is true, I will ask God that love be the starting and ending of all I do, and everything in between. God is love; may my life be a vessel of that Love until He takes me Home.

18 THE ROMANCE OF MINISTRY

Serving Jesus is the most incredible, adventurous, life-changing thing in the world. Ministry is like no other work in the world!

And, ministry is heartache, and stress, and failure, and rejection, and misunderstanding, and financial insecurity, and despair and loneliness and did I mention rejection?

Want to sign up?

You know, writing a newsletter to let people know what you're doing is a real challenge in honesty and faith. I've been writing them since 1975. SO many years! And, I've been reading others' newsletters for all those years. They vary in scope and style, from church bulletins of varying creativity or blandness, to prophetic bombshells (David Wilkerson) to deeply moving heart letters. Then, there came the Madison Avenue ones. "We are in a CRISIS! The devil and I are in the BOXING RING!" (Complete with a graphic art depiction of the Evangelist and an ugly demon.) Everything was a crisis - bold print, italics - and underlined in RED.

At first, I was impressed, because my name was in the letter, several times!

Then came "The" letter which shattered my naiveté:

"Dear Mrs. G. Reit,

You are one of our dearest friends! Without your immediate gift of $1,000, we won't make it, Mrs. G. Reit!"

Not an exact reading, but close. Well, I'm not married, and I'm male. So I figured the letter was a fraud.

That's when I learned big ministries were paying big-name Washington political firms multiple thousands of dollars to write and send those letters, red ink and personalized. One secular magazine showed a politician's pre-fab mass mailing letter, and it was exactly the same as the ministry pre-fab letters I'd received. It was disheartening.

Then, of course, came product newsletters; splinters from the cross

Jesus died on, even a piece of Jewish lamb's wool, which if you placed your hand on it would heal you. It was sickening.

As for me, I've learned slowly. My early letters were filled with too much jargon and painted a rosy picture than belied the internal struggle behind the work. Then, in reading Amy Carmichael's books, I found a heart I could identify with. She deliberately turned away from writing the kinds of newsletters missionaries sent and supporters expected: only positive reports, glowing with news of salvations and victories. She would come to be criticized for her realistic, honest portrayals of life on the mission field. She called her letter, "Things As They are."

And so, in 1990 or so, my "Where I Live" newsletters became "Things As They Are," and I've tried to write honestly, without compromise, without flourish, frill or hidden things. I value Paul's words about renouncing hidden things of dishonesty. It's important to me.

That's not to say I haven't thrown a few letters out. After all, what would you think if I wrote,

"Dear Friends,

I've had it. I'm broke. The kids are making me crazy. I don't eat, I don't sleep, and I'm getting fat and old. Pray for me, I'm running away..."

Well, somewhere in between that and "everything's glorious" I hope I'm striking a good balance. Some of your letters tell me I'm getting there. I try to stay honest and hopeful too, real but also full of promise for the future. Even though I throw out a few letters that may be deemed too negative, I still hope to one day be bold enough to write and send out articles on "The Eternal Sheephood of Some Believers" and "Parishioners That Abuse."

Words are powerful. And even in my attempts at honesty, I find we all have an inborn tendency to romanticize the ministry from both sides of it - those who do it, and those who wish they could. Someone with a 9 to 5 job, a family and a relatively uneventful life can easily read or hear about front-line work and think two things: One: "That's got to be so exciting! I'd love to be doing that!" And two: "My life is so meaningless. I'll never be able to do something significant for God."

These precious folks need to know that everyone is called to ministry. The best and most real work of God, in my opinion, is done with you in your workplace, family and circle of friends and neighbors. I often long for the real life, daily contact and opportunity to share Jesus with people the "ministry" excludes me from!

Second, yes, the "ministry" can be exciting. It's also, and more often, trudge, boredom, paperwork, isolation, loneliness and frustration. It's about divisive people and petty concerns and meaningless distractions and endless delays.

My writings are as real as I can make them. There are victories - great ones. The kids and young folk here can say things that are so eternal that I weep. Then you get a phone message from one you loved who left God, one you loved more than life, who became bitter and you find yourself being called the lowest, hypocritical scum and a flurry of other nonprintable, hateful insults (on a phone message, of course, so you have no defense) and you cry, and ask why, and want to quit! You failed and they hate you for failing them and suddenly every good and precious thing you gave and shared is trampled and forgotten. No heartbreak equals this kind.

The romance is shattered; but you can't quit, because it's in your blood. And, there's the one who writes and says, "I won't let you or Jesus down." And that's the terrifying, confusing reality of real ministry.

More than one has come to us to help, full of romance about ministry and kids. They felt, as I once did, that hugs and kisses and love could conquer all. They don't. Once I put my hand on a young lady's shoulder after she'd thanked me for being such a good pastor. And she slapped me - in front of everyone! I did not know she was walking through a memory of being molested. It was devastating, but I said nothing, crying alone later - after everyone left. That's ministry! It tests and brings out all you are, for good or for bad, the hidden stuff of the heart.

Others have left after realizing the ministry is 95% perspiration, 5% inspiration. It costs everything. It's real life, conflicts, sleeplessness, grueling prayer. It costs everything! It takes teamwork, obedience, guts, faithfulness and a no-surrender heart.

I've recently been shown that there is a generation of kids and children who are so numb, battered, abused and angry that hugs, love and warmth won't cure them. Only faithful love and time, honesty and truth, and endurance can heal these wounded hearts. You'll endure insults, blasphemy, failure, rejection, anger and betrayal. But then, one will grab on to God and make it real, and he will heal, and if there's romance to this work, that's it.

For the one. No matter how bloody the battle. No matter how long it takes.

Only brave hearts need apply.

19 WINDOWS

While the whole world, periodically, waits for the latest Windows computer update, God has been talking to me about other kinds of windows. I wasn't expecting it. I was praying one morning about our work with the youth here, and the Lord said, "They need a window more than a mirror. Be a window to them."

"Without a vision, the people cast off restraint." (Prov. 29:18)

We have become a people so self-centered that we can't see beyond ourselves. I believe in God's healing, inside and out. But I've seen, over the years, believers becoming so bent on "fixing" themselves - fixing their marriages, fixing their careers and personal lives, that many are left with one burning question: "Why? What's it for? What's next?" In frustration, many "cast off restraint" because they have no vision - not for themselves, not for their church, not for their families. And so they dry up and die inside. We need a vision!

You see, God does want to heal us from our brokenness. He does want our families restored. But do you know why? Well, first, because He loves us, He wants to set us free. But what is freedom for? "To serve one another in love." (Gal. 5:13) Too many of us grab healing, then like the lepers Jesus healed, trot off happily. Few of us are like the one who returned to Jesus in thankfulness to say, "What can I do for You?"

There are many people I know who are so distraught with their sins and weaknesses that they feel they will never be useful to God. And unfortunately, others can hold up the Big Mirror to them and say, "See? See what you did? See what you're like?" It is possible to be so self-focused on our sins and failures that we lose hope. Isn't that essentially what Paul was trying to convey? Freedom can't come from the law. The law is the straight-edge to show us how crooked we are, to bring us to Christ. It's the mirror to show how hopeless without Him we are. "It is evident that no man is justified by the works of the Law..." (Gal. 3:11) If the law is the mirror, showing us in all the ugliness and bluntness possible our true sinful condition, then Jesus is our Window. He's freedom from the mirror!

You see, most of the kids and people I know are well aware of their failures and sins. Sometimes they need a mirror of truth, usually when they are blind and their hearts stray. But the mirror is a wake-up call, not a sledge hammer. They need not just confrontation but answers, deliverance. The law doesn't provide that. They need a vision. Self-help is OK, discipline is necessary, but folks, if all Jesus gave Peter was a promise that he'd be a new and improved fisherman, the sermon at Pentecost would have never happened. Peter needed to see beyond himself. Beyond the sea of Galilee to the sea of lost humanity and to see himself as a vision-filled soul-catcher. The mirror of failure returns us to what we are and were. "I'm going back to fishing, it's no use!", Peter said after facing his denial of his Lord and the loss of his expectations and vision. Jesus came - forgave what Peter faced in the mirror of failure - but not only! He gave him a window! "See out there, Peter? Sheep! I want you to feed them!" From failure to fulfillment – from mirror to meaning - from vacillation to vision - from self to Christ!

Jesus was saying to Peter, as he wants to say to you: "I know, and you know, what you are. But I know what you can be - what you will be - what I want you to be!" It's a pointing away from ourselves into the limitless purposes of God for our lives. We can do anything, be anything He asks.

But we've got to have a vision that goes beyond ourselves into Him. Not one great Bible hero was not faced with the mirror of law and truth - and faced their own spiritual bankruptcy, failure and sinful hopelessness. They came to the end of themselves - and found Him. In that moment of despair, they laid down the mirror of self-exposure and cried out to the Living God for mercy. And He gave them a window! "Abraham, look at the stars. More than them will be your descendants. Moses, you failed me. Still I will make you a deliverer. David, you committed great sins. But out of your failure and repentance will come Solomon, your heir, and forefather to the Messiah." He never exposes just to wound, but so we can surrender and grab onto His power to transform us!

"The strength of sin is the law." (1 Cor. 15:56) The strength of failure is the mirror of self-reflection, self-improvement and self-centeredness. God needs to get us to see beyond. As I was praying, this is what I saw: (Keep in mind the mirror being the law and the window being relationship with Jesus):

A mirror is a reflection of oneself. A window is a vision beyond oneself.

A mirror only reflects what's there. A window reflects what's OUT there.

Mirrors point out flaws. Windows point to promises of deliverance.

A mirror is limited. A window is limitless.

A mirror says, "Look at you." A window says, "Look at that!" and "look at Him!"

A mirror is a harsh, unforgiving, unyielding surface. A window is a transparent wonder.

A mirror lets you see yourself. A window lets you see others - and Jesus.

A mirror is fixed, allowing nothing in, or out. A window lets out heat, staleness and lets in cool, fresh air.

A mirror speaks of the failure of yesterday and the hopelessness of today. A window speaks of the hope of tomorrow, and eternity.

A mirror is a rebuke. A window is a vision.

Yes, there's a time for the mirror of truth and facing ourselves. But not for self-defeating, visionless purposes, but to ask God to search our hearts, deliver us from the self-centered quest for self-improvement into deliverance to His vision for our lives.

Lord, when I'm a mirror I reflect back so much junk to others. But more than knowing what's wrong with them, people need to see a way out - something beyond them - that they matter - that their life matters to You. Lord, we're all sick of day-to-day existing. Your heart is about joy, creativity, fruit-bearing, promise, vision, peace, purpose. We too often live in defeat, depression, loss, conflict, emptiness, death, selfishness and fear. Lord, we are a stagnant pool. Can You plow a channel of Life into the stagnant pool of our hearts, for fresh water to flow? Show us how. Teach us. You are to me life, newness, promise, possibility, dreams, visions, joy, and fresh rain and rainbows, green grass and swaying Eucalyptus, and children laughing and playing and clear cool water and waterfalls. You are love, and embrace, and safety, and tears, not just of sorrow but of relief and belonging. You are crisp fall and crimson sunsets, You are sweet sleep and acceptance, freedom, and Life. LIFE! Heaven. Peace. You are my Window. I love you.

Window

I'd rather have a window than a mirror;
To see outside instead of seeing me.
I'd rather see beyond to possibilities
Than just myself, and therefore, selfishly

I'd rather have a window than a mirror
Not vanity, but freedom from these walls
I'd rather risk the wilds and woods and open skies
Than remain forever trapped within these halls

A mirror shows me all I know I really am,
As well as everything I'll never be
But a widow takes me out beyond these limitings
To places hearts of children can be free

So I'd rather have a window than a mirror,
Though mirrors serve a purpose, that is true;
But windows are the door to every promise
A step away from my heart, into You.

20 AFTER CHRISTMAS MESSSAGE

I love Jesus for the way He just drops truth into your heart when you least expect it. This Christmas, 2 things came to me that really opened my heart a little more to His. So, in the midst of used present wrappings and a brittle Christmas tree, sit with me for a moment and hear.

The first came from a story sent to me about children in a Christmas play. A young boy, playing the Innkeeper in Bethlehem, had just one line: "There's no room in the Inn." But he was so touched at the forlorn faces of "Joseph and Mary" as they walked away, he quickly added, "Don't go, Joseph! You and Mary can have MY room!"

It took a child to teach me about true compassion, about true Christian MISSION. For at the heart of the Gospel, at the heart of who Jesus is in us, is this: "The love of Christ compels me." Don't go, Joseph and Mary. You can have MY room! Sacrificial love born of God's compassion. Jesus said, "I was hungry, you didn't feed me, naked, you didn't clothe me, in prison, you didn't visit me..." But how, WHEN, Jesus? "You didn't do it to the least of these, brothers. You didn't do it to Me." Don't go, Jesus! You can take MY room. You can have MY coat! You can eat MY food.

People dying of AIDS. Homeless folks. Abused kids. Hurt teens. Old people in rest homes, abandoned and forgotten all. Don't go, Jesus! You can have MY room! So much of the church is paralyzed, angry, political, self-serving and utterly selfish. But until we learn to see Jesus in the lost and the hurting, we'll never understand why we're here. Reconciliation. Redemption. "Don't go, Jesus. You can have my room."

The second revelation came at a Christmas play a friend's kids were in. I think every Christian should go to a children's Christmas play - especially the sour-faced, bah-humbug, "it's a pagan holiday!" lot. These plays are WONDERFUL. Know why? They're so earnest. So innocent. So flawed! I relish every sour note, every missed cue, every flubbed line. Know why? First, because these kids have put their whole hearts into making their parents proud. Know why else?

Because they're us! And there's my revelation. It's a perfect picture of the church! Folks, we're so serious and somber and right and determined about everything moral, political and doctrinal. Some of that's OK. But I saw in this children's play a little of God's heart toward us.

You see, God is the ultimate Parent, and He's come to see the production of our lives we're putting on for Him!

Now, I'm sure a few parents, dysfunctional and perfectionistic to the core, winced at every error their child made, returning home with them saying, "You could have done better," or worse, just an icy silence that says volumes about their disappointment in their child's less than perfect performance. And many of us see God like that, don't we? Nothing's good enough. I have to do better, then He'll really love me. What a tragedy! Because God is really seen in the eyes of the parents at that play whose eyes shone with proud tears as they watched their child stumble earnestly over their parts, and after, hugged and kissed them and said, "I'm so proud of you!".

A perfect production? Not by a mile. Not in the play; not in our lives; not in the church! But I believe God watches PROUDLY every stumbling effort we make to walk with Him. Isn't every child longing to hear, "I'm proud of you!"? Isn't that REALLY what the last, "Well done, good and faithful servant" is all about? Do you really believe God is *less* than a human parent, who doesn't focus on the messed up lines but sees only the HEART of their child?

Therein lies the mystery of the church. Christ in us - in humanity - failing, broken, weak, but EARNEST in wanting to please Him! What a MARVEL!

"The church is full of hypocrites." No. The church is full of children.

In the play I watched, the announcer said, "Listen carefully. THEY'VE PUT THEIR WHOLE HEARTS INTO THIS even if they don't speak very loud. Remember, these are children playing adult roles." Adults we are - but to God, we're children taking on adult roles! Can't we stop criticizing and judging each other, and listen, because we're putting our whole hearts into this thing of life in Jesus? Yes, the scriptures speak about putting away CHILDISH things, not being children in understanding, not being children swayed by every wind of doctrine, but can't you also know that to be child-like, to be as a child in trust, in innocence, in wonder and love, is the Father's greatest joy in us? Just to see that we're giving it 100% of our hearts?

Mid-play, there was a start, lines spoken, and then the director came out and interrupted - all was not ready. "Bear with us," she says. "We're all family here, right?" Right! Why can't we? Church life, folks, is messy, filled with interrupted starts, unpreparedness, sins and errors. But bear with each other, we're family! The problem with human plays, as with the church, is you always have prima-donnas who think they're better and don't mind stepping on people, full of pride and arrogance - and you have one-man shows who don't believe anyone is more important than them - and those who say, "I don't want to play with that person. I don't like that person." and those who say, "I don't like my PART." So much like us. But with a play, as with His church, each line, no matter how small, is important to the success of things. And if we're being like Jesus, then we HELP each other - we whisper the missed lines to our friend - we show them where to stand - we encourage them to do their level best. We need EACH PART - each person. To be content with our place in His church because HE knows how important it is, is the greatest source of contentment we can have.

In the play, a child playing a homeless believer is telling the Christmas story, and he's recruiting other homeless friends to act out the story. He looked at some thieving street kids: "Go on! Be Shepherds!" And so, they put on robes and acted the parts. And I saw we Shepherds of God's flock - called out of filth and sin and failure - and God saying to us, "Go on, be Shepherds!" Why, because we're qualified, or better, or gifted? No - because He told us we could, he said, "Go on, then, care for my people." And so we take on robes of righteousness and discard our sinful, thieving past and obey. It's just like that.

I was probably one of the only ones who laughed (or even noticed) when the verse was read, "And they fell down and worshipped Him," and a loud clunk-clunk was heard backstage, which was, apparently, the sound of someone missing a step and falling in the dark backstage. Well, however God gets us to fall down and worship, so be it! But it tied into something another friend told me about their Christmas play, when he was leading some elderly choir members from the dark backstage into the light onstage. They all grabbed his robe and let him lead them out in the darkness. And I saw what faith is really about. The darkness of trials can be so horrific at times, but I fear we are looking for the wrong thing. "God I need an answer. I need miracles. I need results. I need to see where I'm going!" Those elderly ladies backstage only needed someone to lead them through the dark. We only need to cling to Jesus in the dark of our trials! So faith is not just what you believe; it's who you are clinging to and holding on to!

After the play, I watched a child on stage, alone, in the dim after-light of the night, touching the props, face filled with wonder because he'd been chosen to be part of this. And I thought, won't this be it, on the final day? To have been part of this Grand Production of life in Christ, to have worked together, fought together and with each other, sweat and earnestly tried to be all God asked, and then to feel our Father's embrace and hear, "Well done, little one. I'm so proud of you!" and then to stand and look back, and touch the props and circumstances, failures and missteps and successes and memories and people in our earthly lives, and with the eyes of a child, to feel the awe and wonder of it all, that we were chosen to play at all? That through our failed cues, missteps and sins, still we saw the glistening tears of pride in our Father's eyes - not because we did it perfectly - but because we put our whole hearts into this - into Him?

And really, that's all that matters.

God bless us, every one.

21 THE LAME PRINCE

I finally found out who I am.

Maybe I always knew...I just hadn't seen it in black and white before.

I already had my message ready for the youth service in Oklahoma City...sort of...as much as I'm ever ready. Okay, I had a scrap of paper with a few notes. My message was going to be about Jonathan's crippled son, Mephibosheth.

And you think YOU have a funny name.

It could've been worse. In fact I could almost write a book about parents who name their kids unkind things. Example: Governor Hogg of Texas who named his daughters Ima and Ura. Example: My mother's friends in Salt Lake City growing up: Iona and Harry Legg. I was told (but I cannot prove) that the man who created the Lear Jet named his daughter Crystal Shanda. I even knew a hippie kid in California growing up whose two brothers were named (I'm not making this up) WinterSpring SummerFall and Sunshine Siddartha. The obvious nicks being Winnie and Sunnie. I think criminal negligence charges would not be unreasonable so these kids could have free therapy for life.

I really like name books, and I think it's neat, especially for kids, to know that their name means something, and what it is. Unless of course their name means "Swampy bog" or something. I kind of like the Native American idea of naming kids after things they do or represent, like "Dances with Wolves." At this stage of my work I'd like to be called "wrestles with ostriches." But in fact I love my name and thank God my parents chose it for me: Gregory Robert. It means "Faithful Watchman," and I pray I will always live up to that name.

My last name is another matter. I don't care for being named after a piece of marsh bamboo, but believe me it could have been much much worse.

My dad's real name was Foote. There are different stories as to why Pop changed it. Neither my grandma nor my step grandma liked my Pop much, so I'm not sure either is a reliable story. But one said that back in the forties they called police officers "flat foot" and Mother wouldn't put up with that if they were to marry so he changed it.

The other is that mother refused to marry, have kids, and have people saying, "Why, here comes Mrs. Foote and all her little Feet!" Who knows, really. I'm just *so* thankful he changed it regardless of why.

Names identify us, they differentiate us from others. They tell us we are unique. Biblical Hebrew names, especially, were full of meaning.

Which is why I love the story of Mephibosheth. His name meant "Dispeller of Shame."

The fact is he was an object of shame - at least to himself - to his family and friends. You see, Mephibosheth's father was David's lifelong friend - Jonathan. And his father's father was King Saul. Mephibosheth's dad was supposed to be king after his grampa died. Instead, his father Jonathan and his grampa Saul were both killed on the same day. While running from the coming battle, Mephibosheth's nurse accidentally dropped him and he became permanently "lame in his feet." (2 Samuel 4:4).

He was the Lame Prince.

I didn't make up that name. When I was in Oklahoma for the youth service I sat in the pastor's office praying, asking God if He was sure I was supposed to talk about this story - when I saw a book the pastor had written lying on the table - "The Lame Prince." The story of Mephibosheth. I knew I had heard God right. I also was strangely filled with an understanding that I, too, am God's Lame Prince. I will explain that more in a moment.

Mephibosheth must have felt a thousand things growing up. He was an orphan. David had become King, a place his grandpa had, that his father should have had, and eventually he himself. Instead he was probably in hiding for his life, because new kings tended to kill off all the remaining family members of the outgoing King.

He must have thought his name was a joke. "Dispeller of Shame." And here he was - lame, exiled, abandoned. Nothing BUT shame had been his life. Don't you think he was bitter? Angry? Wounded? I think he was. There David was, King - while he sat alone and shamed. The Lame Prince.

David was now King. All was at peace. All his enemies were subdued. He must have been thinking about Jonathan, his dearest friend. He must have ached to think of him gone. Once in a lifetime does a friendship like that happen.

No one could ever replace Jonathan.

"Is there still anyone left of the house of Saul, that I may show him kindness for Jonathan's sake?", David asked. (2 Samuel 9:1) There was. His name was Mephibosheth. He was brought to David.

What must he have thought? That this was it, the end? Had David brought him to finish the job? But instead of death, David said, "Don't be afraid, son. I brought you here to give you back what your grandfather lost. I want you to live here. I want you to eat at my table all your life. I want to take care of you."

"What is your servant, that you should look upon such a dead dog as I?" Mephibosheth replied. He could not believe - lame and rejected as he had been all his life - that instead of death - he was asked to come and live in the King's House forever.

You bet I understand that story.

A little later in the story, Mephibosheth tells David, "You are like the angel of God."

You know, I wish we could really grasp all this. You and I were wounded, rejected, angry, bitter, lame sinners who knew somehow we were born for something but we didn't know what. And the King said, "I want them to come and live in My House." What wonderful, undeserving grace that would bring us to His very own House and give us His royal Name!

Mephibosheth, in the end, really WAS the "dispeller of shame." It happened because someone sought him out and brought him Home.

I have always believed that the message of God's love was "for the one." I'm not into crowds. I want to find the one.

I went to church camp many summers ago, my first time since 1974. It was at Mountain Aire, New Mexico. Doesn't that sound exotic, refreshing, doesn't it evoke wonderful thoughts of fresh breezes, waterfalls?

It was two trees and a mound of dirt. No river. No kidding. Lots of dust. Mountian Aire, my foot.

Mine was close to the worst behaved cabin at camp, perhaps in camp history. God knew who to pick to shepherd them though, I, who had quit boy scouts at twelve in a fit of rebellion.

We got busted for breaking curfew the first night. Ritalin wouldn't have helped that gig.

The next day, the Fearless Leader of these "bunk rats" as they named themselves, got fired - from volunteer sausage serving. I didn't know you could get fired for a non-paying job, but I did. News spread fast. The next day a little boy looked at me sadly and said, "Mister, I'm sorry you got fired from sausages." It was pathetic, really. I'm not cut out to be an athletic camp leader, especially if I can't even hang on to a sausage job. Nevertheless, I knew I was at this camp for a reason. There were Mephibosheths here.

Two of my campers were brought to me with lots of instructions - mainly, with medical directions on how to make sure they got their medicine. They were big kids. They wouldn't be playing any reindeer games, I assure you. And my heart was struck. No one was going to mess with these boys. No one was going to tease them or humiliate them on my watch - I remembered too well both the long nights trying to breathe and the days I cried and begged not to go to school because I couldn't take the humiliation and teasing anymore. I learned these boys' names - all of them - but especially these two. They both had an evident call of God on them. Remember what I said earlier about the importance of names? Well, it's not just our given names that affect us but what others call us. Life and death is in the power of the tongue, and you can wound or heal with your words. So, so many kids remember the anguish of being called "stupid," "fat," "loser," "half-wit," and on it goes. And a lot of the kids I've loved and known got that from home as well as school. We may be lame of heart, mind, or body - but we stay lame of spirit because we can't forget those awful words spoken by the proud and insensitive. The mold us into what we think of ourselves - what we become.

So besides making sure no one called these boys names, I did everything I could to bolster their hearts in God's way. I told them how great they were, how proud I was of them. One of them flawlessly sang worship in sign language with me during the night services - who would have known, based on outward appearance, that this big kid had such a profound gift, such an eloquent voice of hands and heart? And the other boy - I called him "Pastor David" every time I saw him, because he had the tender heart of a shepherd only the wounded healers have - and he WILL be a pastor. I just know.

What an awesome moment at the last day when the speaker asked all the kids who felt God had called them to ministry to stand, "Pastor David" rise without hesitation to respond to that call. I expect to see him in a profound place of ministry someday. I pray he will remember - not me, but that "someone" looked out for him and did not ridicule him but made him feel special - someone who even called him "Pastor."

And it's not just the rejected and weak that need our kindness. There are plenty of Mephibosheths on honor rolls, who are well off, who are good looking and excel in sports and appear to have it all. I spoke with a preacher's kid that last afternoon. Nothing special; just taking an interest in his young life.

After the last service, I saw him sitting alone on top of a monkey bars near the commissary. I said something briefly to him going by, and then suddenly something caught my eye - a single, solitary tear coming down his face. I stopped dead in my tracks, and asked him to come down and talk. Instead he came down and grabbed me and sobbed for the longest time. Through his tears all I heard was, "Thank you for being my friend." This was a hurting, limping Mephibosheth in a preacher's kid's body, just needing a friend.

Folks, I'm nothing special except to God and maybe my friends. But I do know how to see kids on the inside. And I am always humbled when they accept the only gifts I can give: Jesus, and my faith in their lives and hearts and callings.

Camp just reminded me: This is who I am. This is all I am.

And I am so because someone, so many years ago, was my King David. He was just a little guy in a big LTD that picked me up, and instead of seeing a scarred, angry, messed up, demonized mess of a kid, he saw - a Prince. How? How could he, except he saw through Jesus' eyes? He kept on me - kept praying - kept calling - until I surrendered to Jesus and the King brought this Lame Prince into His own Home forever.

There were King Davids along the way - after I became a believer - who loved me, spent time with me and called me the names God wanted me to have - son - loved - called - special - and I remember them all - Dave Malkin - Doris - Ted - Mike and Rita - Claudette and Rosemary - Rick - I could go on for pages. Each elevated me out of my limping heart into a place of dignity and purpose. Next to Jesus, I owe them my heart.

And I have always asked, and longed, to be that to others.

You see, I still limp. The scars of my youth and childhood were deep and wide, both physically and emotionally. Some would chide me and say, "Don't confess that limp!" Listen, I know who I am. I am not deceiving myself. There are many things I will never know and can never be. And so, so many scars still sting from the corridors of my past. And I want it that way. Yes, God could take away even the slightest "limp." But I'm not sure I want that. I WANT those scars to be tender to the touch, so that Pastor Davids, and preacher's kids, and hurting children do not escape my sight but instead capture my heart and my prayers - because in my healing, I can still feel the pang of what it was like to be rejected, bitter, alone. I want those scars to be a bridge they can walk over to find the King's waiting arms and welcoming banquet set out for the royalty they are, if only they could see themselves as He sees.

I will never forget last year in a moment of self-doubt and discouragement, driving west to California across the desolate New Mexico highway and saying, "Jesus, was it worth it what You did for me? Have I given you anything at all with my life that made it worth it for You to die for me, has anything I have done even come close to thanking You for saving me?" The answer was unexpected and reduced me to tears. "Son," He said gently, "Every one You have loved, You loved for Me."

"You were an angel of God," Mephibosheth told David.

And so are you, and so am I. And Jesus is counting on our arms, and our hands, and our words, and our kindnesses, and our time and our best love to find the Mephibotheths of this world, this generation - find them, love them, bring them to forgiveness at the Cross of Jesus, and bring them into Father's House forever. My loved friend, we are so focused on the whys of our lives, our hurts, our pasts. Why did they die? Why did he leave? Why did she hurt me? Why was I always ill?

But the real, life-changing prayer is not "Why?", a question that will never answer your questions nor heal your wounds: It is "Father, WHAT FOR?" Nothing is for nothing. Your limp is not for nothing. Your history - painful as it is - your unique failures and rejections and losses - are for something. There is a Mephibosheth that you will see, and you will know is hurting, like no one else can know because you know his agony, you have walked through her sorrow and loss - and YOU are the angel of God to them. Find them. Don't waste your sorrows. Use them. Seek out the broken and battered along the highway who will be forgotten forever if you do not care, if you do not see the wings of God that bring you to their side to say, "Come, Prince, come Princess; come Home to Father's House. He wants you to be His forever."

I finally understand who I am. I'm a Lame Prince. And I would rather be that than the most able and blessed person on earth. For in that weakness that was my past redeemed by Jesus, I have also become a shepherd to His broken lambs.

What more blessed calling could their possibly be?

And Pastor David – if you somehow read this, know that I have never stopped praying for you. You were always a prince in God's eyes, and in mine.

Gregory R Reid

22 THE BIRTH OF COMPASSION

I've always contended that, if I hadn't become a Christian, I would have become the most selfish person on the face of the earth. Sometimes I still think I am. My mother certainly thought so, and when I got out of Bible School, she sat me down and point-blank told me so. Ouch. Mom was never much for flattery. She was right, if a little extreme. I've been blessed to be in ministry for four decades. If that doesn't knock the selfishness out of you, nothing will.

We do have kind of a mistaken idea about our character, though. Most of us believe that when we come to Christ, our pasts not only are obliterated, but none of it matters, good or bad.

Paul did not share this idea. He referred to both bad things (killing Christians) and good (sitting at Gamaliel's feet) as part of what made up the person he became. God often uses the bad of our experiences - and the good - even before Christ - to be the octave that speaks into someone's life.

God puts to death our old sin nature but does not annihilate our character and personality. Insightful, quiet and melancholic people aren't turned into Robin Williams. Upbeat, funny, sunshine morning types get saved, and usually remain upbeat, funny, sunshine morning types.

Joseph's youthful dreams and gentle heart became a leader's vision and compassionate character in rulership.

Peter's flamboyant, aggressive nature was refined in affliction and became the tools of a fiery preacher.

God takes out the bad and sinful and destructive and builds on the soul He created at birth, and strengthens the good character stuff we picked up even before we knew Christ.

As children, we are burdened by the inevitable blossoming of sin, and then sin's consequence, death - but we are also shaped and molded by circumstances, people and things - and these are things that God will redeem when we give our lives to Him.

For me, when you added my capacity for selfishness to sin-in-bloom, my potential for egotistical, hateful behavior was huge.

But for God.

Even before I knew Him, He birthed compassion in me. And his name was Danny DeLeonard.

I was about the shyest, most fragile kid in grade school. No one picked me for softball, because I threw "like a girl." I hated recess and avoided getting picked on by hiding in the corner with the kid everyone called "retard" who I knew wouldn't hurt me.

When I was about nine, I had some painful dental work. The dentist had a bowl of kids' rings to give to kids after their appointment. I picked one with a yellow "stone".

My mistake was wearing it to school the next day. During recess, someone saw the ring and within minutes, it seemed like all the bullies in the school had surrounded me. "Look!" they taunted. "He's wearing a GIRL'S ring!" "Look at this sissy boy!" another one yelled, and they started to shove me around, and I was scared to death, and crying.

"Hey!" I heard an angry voice shout, and like a blur, a redheaded kid jumped in running and started to shove the kids back hard. "Leave him alone!!" "He's got a girls' ring!" one of them protested. The redheaded kid, whose name was Danny (I knew he was about the toughest kid in school) shoved his fist underneath the nose of the other kid while grabbing him by the shirt and making him look. "SO WHAT? Look at MY ring! You think I've got a girl's ring, man? HUH?" "N...no!" the other kid said, shaking now. "Yeah I didn't think so." All the kids skulked away, leaving just Danny and me. I couldn't believe it - 11 year old Danny DeLeonard defended ME! "Thanks", I said shyly. "Don't worry 'bout them," he grinned. "I got a ring just like yours!" And he walked away. I'd just found my first hero.

Danny planted a seed of compassion in my heart. Because of that inexplicable act of kindness, two things happened.

One, I can no longer remember the names and faces of the vast armies of bullies that tormented me from grade school to Junior High. They stopped mattering. They stopped making a lasting impression on me, all because one person thought I was worth defending.

Two, my heart began to feel the hurt of other kids who were rejected, cast out, ridiculed. Before, it was just my hurt, and I just crawled off into a corner to bleed. But God had sent Danny DeLeonard to place the seed of compassion in my heart, and it grew, and I found myself drawn toward the outcasts.

Eileen was in the 4th grade and had coke-bottle thick glasses. One day the kids circled her like sharks when the teacher was out and started calling her "four eyes." The feeding frenzy intensified until they got the desired result - she broke down and cried in humiliation and shame. It fed their tormenting until she cried out, "Today's my birthday!" and sobbed uncontrollably. Dead silence. The criminals were caught and shamed by their own cruelty. And I felt an ache I'd never felt for anyone but myself - my heart was breaking for her. I caught her on the playground. "Don't worry about them," I said quite imitating my hero, Danny DeLeonard "Happy birthday, Eileen." "Yeah, happy birthday" a couple others said. She smiled through her tears. "Thank you," she said, wiping her tears away. Was kindness and compassion that simple? Did I do for her what Danny did for me? Would she remember the sweetness of a kid who was kind in a moment the whole world was cruel? I hope so. Either way, the die was cast. That little bit of God's heart toward the outcast began to grow in me.

Suddenly, I felt drawn toward kids like Eileen...like me...

Danny T. was a tiny, skinny, scared kid. So, so abused, I knew it even then. So I tried my best to be his friend. But with brutally abusive alcoholic parents, dirt-poor conditions and no safe refuge, he was almost already gone, even at eight. I was devastated - but not surprised - to learn he had brutally murdered two girls at age 17, and is to this day locked up as one of California's most dangerous prisoners. Too little kindness...too late. How many Danny T.'s are in our schools today?

Timmy was also in my 4th grade class. A sadder kid I'd never seen. He never talked, never smiled. His clothes were old and worn. Timmy was the brunt of every evil taunt from every cruel kid at school. One day while the teacher was distracted, a group of little devils had begun verbally hacking into Timmy until he finally cried out, "Leave me alone! I can't help the way I dress! My father's a drunk!" He ran out of the room sobbing. The mob, so typical, got what they wanted, then went dead silent when they actually got it.

What they didn't expect was the wrath of our teacher, Mr. Chestley. He was a very tall, imposing and normally very nice man. But today, he strode over to these evil little children and started yelling at them. The shock on their faces was priceless. "Don't you EVER make fun of that boy again!" he practically screamed. "You have NO IDEA what he goes through at home! One more stunt like that and you're ALL going to the principal's office! Am I CLEAR?!?" Heck yeah, he was clear! They understood - and so did I. Our School had a Champion for hurt kids, and I had an adult hero. I wanted to be just like him.

I got my chance on a two day scout hike when I was twelve. The hike was hell, and I kept wondering if the scoutmasters had Nazi armbands in their backpacks for after-hours training. Equating a ten-mile hike with character building, I disagreed after six miles of torturous uphill walking, and I managed to pull off an all-troop sit-down strike. The scoutmasters blinked, and we set up camp at the top of the San Bernardino Mountains.

Chris was a little guy, probably just eleven, skinny, shy and wearing glasses. He slept between me and another kid, the three of us settled into our sleeping bags under the glorious star-strewn sky. But I did not sleep, because Chris moaned, cried out and whimpered all night in his sleep. Even at twelve, I knew he was in terrible emotional pain - he was hurt and he was terrified - and tortured inside. I felt a stab in my heart every time he cried out. I felt water in my eyes. I felt helpless.

The next morning we packed out and headed down to the bottom of the canyon, and I, being a bit of a weakling myself, was at the end of the troop line.

As I rounded the final part of the trail, I heard a ruckus - yelling, laughing, and crying - Chris' crying. He was cornered and being shoved by a thirteen-year-old bully I never liked while several other kids stood by and cheered.

Something snapped in me. I ran toward the middle of the fray, screaming, "LEAVE HIM ALONE!!!" and before the 13 year old goon had even a chance to see it coming, I had him on the ground and was pummeling him over and over, screaming primal, unintelligible threats. Three guys dragged me off of him. "Don't you EVER hurt him again, you GOT IT?!?" I screamed, and yes, they all got it. I put my arm around Chris and walked him out of the now silent crowd. "Th..thanks," Chris sniffled, wiping the snot on his flannel shirt sleeve. "It's ok Chris," I said quietly. "Don't worry about them." "Are you my friend? Will you be my friend?" Chris asked hopefully. "Yeah, I'm your friend."

Wherever Chris is, I hope he is strong, and successful, and unafraid. I pray he got healed of whatever hurt him. And I still pray he finds the Lord of Compassion, that, unbeknownst to me at 12, drove this skinny, scared kid into a pack of juvenile hounds and transformed me into a fierce lion for one moment - for one kid.

When I found Jesus, or rather when He found me, He took all of the sinful nature in me, and all the sins and shame, and nailed it to His cross. I wasn't sure there would be anything left of me.

But there was.

As He stripped off the old, layer by layer, much of what I thought was "me" was being taken away - arrogance, fear, rage - (and much still ahead, I am sure) - I felt at times only a shell would remain. To my surprise, a jewel lay shining underneath the rubble. It had been placed years ago and protected by my Father's loving hand, and try though he did, Satan was not able to steal it away. It was compassion.

After so much sin and devastation, I wondered if my new life would be of any value at all. I couldn't even love. I didn't know how.

But when I was sixteen and I met Johnny, a scared, horribly abused 13 year old at church, the gem God had placed in my heart began to burn. In his face I saw Timmy., Eileen and Danny T...and myself. Scared and uncertain, I stepped into Johnny's life and became his friend...another story, written in another book. God gave life to me, and now I knew this was what I longed to give others. I FELT the pain of others. I burned with anger at injustice and the injury of the innocent...the defenseless.

From that gem, God birthed a heart of ministry in me. Though the years have passed, it burns still. Most days, I'm just Joe Average. But if there's a hurting kid, you may find me weeping all night over them, or holding them while THEY weep. Injure a child, and this very average lamb will become a furious lion. I learned it long ago...from a kid named Danny DeLeonard...a teacher named Mr. Chestley...and from the fierce heart of the Lion of Judah Himself. Paul said it best. "Who is weak and I am not weak? Who is offended and I do not burn?" "Rejoice with those who rejoice...and weep with those that weep." That is the heart of real ministry. Bringing God's love to the widow, the orphan, the fatherless and the friendless.

Truly God rebuilds Jerusalem on her ruins. And even in the ravages of our former lives, He redeems it all. I know. And, so does someone else...

It was at Bible School, 1975, three states away from my hometown and all its memories...

...I was lost in worship, my hands raised, singing a gentle song about God's love, when someone next to me interrupted my worship by tapping on my shoulder. "Are you Greg Reid?" he softly asked. I turned. "Timmy?!?" It was Timmy., from almost a lifetime ago, now a healthy, full grown and Jesus-filled Christian! Suddenly we are lost in embraces, laughter, tears. Fifteen years and a world away, suddenly, compassion had come full circle. We had both been touched by a stranger's kindness, a Champion's care.

We had both, mercifully, been captured by God's compassionate love.

23 PRESENT IN THE PAIN

I will never forget the story of the Pastor who was backing out of his driveway on the way to church and accidentally ran over – and killed – his three-year-old child.

It was the first time in my walk that I was confronted with a tragedy that no tidy one-line response could be anything but an obscene insult.

Do you have an answer as to why that tragedy happened? If you had been there, you would have no doubt felt the compulsion to say something to explain it. It is in our nature, because when life is out of control, fear compels us to somehow "grab the wheel" – grab the controls of rational explanation.

Job faced far worse. He lost all his family except his wife. And she was no help! Although, we tend to criticize her for telling Job to "curse God and die" (she was wrong) – and we don't considering the agony of a loved one who watches her mate suffer beyond belief and is helpless to stop it – not considering it was her children who died too – not considering that her reply was in any event, more human and more honest than Job's friends.

There is an important modern life similarity to how we handle extreme tragedy as believers. So many people in the throes of horrendous anguish of loss and suffering, death and bereavement, speak out of their rage, their overwhelming hurt, their sense of violation. "Why did God do this? I hate Him! I wish I were dead!"

And, in rush "Job's friends" to encircle and pontificate and tell them, "You shouldn't be saying those things! Don't you know God is a good God?"

Yes, He is – beyond our wildest dreams – which is why these observing "wise" people aren't incinerated on the spot for their arrogance in correcting people in their pain. We deny bleeding hearts permission to feel, to cry, to rage, to scream, to question why. Unless you have suffered such a loss, you cannot grasp how it feels – like a helpless butterfly, stuck through the heart with a pin, your wings of hope ripped off as you agonize in complete helplessness and terror.

Rather than provide quick, easy answers to the person's pain-blinded outcries, we would do well to do what Job's friends did at first: "No one said a word to him, for they saw that his grief was very great." (Job 2:13b)

At some point though, they broke their silence and began an endless series of monologues about why this happened to Job – and how he should – and shouldn't respond.

I think I know part of the reason why they – and we – feel so driven, so compelled to rush in and fill the void of someone's loss with an endless stream of words.

They – and we – were terrified. The silence of exquisite, cruel, seemingly meaningless suffering and loss screams at us: "If it happened to them, a good, godly person, it can happen to me too!" Suddenly we're faced with the reality that godliness is not an immunity from suffering – sometimes incomprehensible suffering.

So we chatter, whistle in the dark, and send forth unrestrained explanations and "reasons" to gain rational control of the event – and to distance them from us, and their suffering as well – (It's because they sinned. They didn't have enough faith. Surely I'm not like them…) We do it to keep their devastation away from our safe, non-suffering world, and to avoid the truth: It COULD be me. It might YET be me.

I came to understand this after my father died. Mom had died two years before; the loss of my father was so overwhelming that I thought I would not survive it. Except for three friends, who did the kindest thing – simply loved and wept with me – the rest neither sat in silence nor offered words. They just…..vanished. Hid. Ignored. I wrote about this in my book, "Silence and the Distance Between Us." "I know why. I'm your future," I wrote. "I am the ghost of Christmas future, the Death Mask…They, too, will face this." Death comes to everyone, and loss; it is easier to just stay away from those who have lost loved ones, because it reminds us that we, too, are not immune.

Some people – a very small handful, will know a minimal amount of suffering in their lives. Many more will suffer illness, loss of employment, stray children, death of parents, a spouse or children, the betrayal of adultery, the agony of molestation.

Some will suffer so profoundly we can only gasp in horror and rend our garments.

But, Christian or not, suffering WILL come. "In the world you will have tribulation. But be of good cheer. I have overcome the world." (John 16:33) And if He did, then so can we. But how? How can we overcome incomprehensible suffering and tribulation?

One word: Emmanuel.

GOD WITH US.

"Are not two sparrows sold for a copper coin? And not one of them falls to the ground apart from the Father's will." (Mt. 10:29. The most accurate translation of this says, 'NOT ONE OF THEM FALLS WITHOUT THE FATHER."

We have misinterpreted this as, "A bird doesn't die without God noticing it."

But doesn't just "notice." "Oh, there goes another bird." No dispassionate calculation: "One down, 3 trillion to go…" Not one falls WITHOUT THE FATHER! Oh, how that speaks to my heart, my deepest pain! It says that Father falls with the sparrow – not observer – but organically, feelingly, painfully intertwined with the suffering and death of this tiny creature! "Don't fear; you are of more value than many sparrows!"

If our Creator-Father, who with one hand strew trillions of stars casually into the cosmos, was so intimately woven into the suffering, gasping last moments of what most see as a "scrap bird" – an annoyance - a plain and numerous and personality-less bird…

…then you must know how infinitely more He feels – knows – experiences – and is intimately involved with your own suffering! He is neither dispassionate nor a divine accountant in your pain, distantly transcribing your every word and action in your agony. He is embracing you, feeling you, kissing your tears and knowing your deepest cry.

Do you believe that?

Something happens in those terrible moments. It is a divine wrestling match - you, screaming to get away from both the pain and the God you think caused or allowed it…

…and God, squeezing you to the floor, not letting you go, shouting, "Let me hold you! I know! I feel ALL that you do! Give me your pain. I will give you…Myself. My healing. My heart."

Suffering is a mystery and I defy anyone to package simple answers for it. But I do know that if Jesus means anything, He means a God who isn't "God sees us" or "God notices" but God with us. Not running from our pain or hiding from it, not judging, just…there. Intimately there in every tear and heart's cry.

The answers to "why" may or may not come. The rain falls on the just and the unjust. Some tragedy is random, senseless and pointless. I do know that in your suffering, you can know without doubt that "God is at work in all things to produce good." (Romans 8:28) And your suffering will become the next sufferer's embrace and kindness of God through human arms. As Amy Carmichael said, "The end will explain all things." I believe that. Trust in God's goodness. Know that He understands the brokenness of your heart and the often angry and bitter words spoken through grief.

But if you can, in your dark night of the soul, embrace Emmanuel – "God with you" – in the end, the need for answers will recede into the real, eternal, unfailing intimate love of our God who has said, "I am with you always."

He is present in your pain.

He is with you in your worst suffering.

He is there to heal even your deepest hurts.

He is Emmanuel.

25 LOOK BACK

I admit – I get very attached to the young people God blesses my life with. It's always been that way. I've never been quite a "pastor in a place" kind of person. I'm kind of a pastor of the heart. Actually, more of a sheepdog than a shepherd.

Youth ministry isn't "ministry" to me – it's giving life – a two-way gift really. I don't see "youth groups" – just young hearts. I do my best to give His Word. But, like Paul, I am also "willing to give my life, so dear are you to me." I don't stop loving them when they are 20 or 30 or 40. What parent does? Because in my heart...I am a parent, a father. God made me that.

I'm watching another generation pass from youth to adulthood this week. These graduations fold back into other years, other kids, other graduations...unique but with the same summer air, flashing cameras, a sky filled with caps and shouts...the same anticipation...the same sadness and goodbyes to friends and childhood.

I showed up at 11P.M. to see our kids off to camp. Happy for them, sad I do not go this year, praying for safety, and for them all to return full of the love of Jesus.

As we gathered and held hands and prayed, each face was etched onto my heart. They will never know what they mean to me.

Because you see, I've had honors enough for a lifetime -commendations, recommendations, even a Doctorate: all I felt undeserved, but all humbling and gratefully taken. They are things given for what I have done.

But my highest honor in my heart is that I am, for reasons I do not grasp, from a generation I am told does not connect with adults, welcomed. Accepted. Counted on. They are part of me. They always will be.

Still, in the excitement of the trip, they all quickly boarded the bus without looking back, without a wave or a handshake or a hug.

Except for one.

You see, none of them, thankfully, had yet to know what has become a permanent part of my later years – that you must cherish each goodbye, because you do not know when it will be your last goodbye. So I always put my heart in my goodbyes.

I stood and watched the kids board with a very special young man I've known since he was sixteen. He's nearly 21 now. I can't ever remember him not being part of my life. I can't imagine him not being in my life, for the rest of my life. It's just like that. He's grown as a young man and grown as a believer. I am so proud of him.

"Here we are, seeing the kids off…" he joked, like we were parents seeing our kids off to college.

Near the bus, one of our kids lingered to say goodbye to his mom. He's a great kid. Smart, funny, sensitive, real. He's going to be somebody special. (They all are.)

As he gave his mom a last hug, he looked back at us. And he walked back to say goodbye, hugging me tight. Because he knows the dark secret. One day he said goodbye to his dad and his dad never came home, taken in an accident. He knows; you can never assume you get another goodbye.

I'm glad he came back. The overwhelming odds were, I'd see them all again in seven days. And we'll make more memories, and I'll watch them grow up, and there will be more goodbyes as they move away, or move on from this wonderful cocoon called "youth group." And like all parents natural and spiritual, I'll stay behind, miss them, and pray, and hope for a call, an e-mail, a letter. My mother used to tell me, "You always hope your kids still need you…just a little." I understand that now. Before Motel 6 made it a commercial, my parents always used to say, "We'll leave a light on for you." It meant, "This is home. You are always welcome here." I've left that light on in my heart for each young life God has blessed me with over the years. Whether 14 or 40 – they can always call or come "home." Sometimes, they do.

And one day, it will be my final bus ride, my last hug, and I will whisper to each in my heart, "I'll leave the light on for you". And in the joys of heaven, I will be looking back – waiting for them to come Home.

ABOUT THE AUTHOR

Gregory Reid is an ordained minister with American Evangelistic Association and holds an honorary Doctorate of Divinity with Logos Graduate School. He has been in ministry since 1975, and has written 11 books: Nobody's Angel, Nehemiah: Rebuilding the Ruins, Redeeming the Devil's Children, Diary of a Devil Hunter, Treasure from the Master's Heart, Silence and the Distance Between Us, Professional's Guide to Occult Crimes, Cry in the Wilderness, Stray Cats and Other Stories, The Color of Pain and Trojan Church.